RUSSIAN UTOPIA

Russian Shorts

Russian Shorts is a series of thought-provoking books published in a slim format. The Shorts books examine key concepts, personalities, and moments in Russian historical and cultural studies, encompassing its vast diversity from the origins of the Kievan state to Putin's Russia. Each book is intended for a broad range of readers, covers a side of Russian history and culture that has not been well-understood, and is meant to stimulate conversation.

Published Titles

Pussy Riot: Speaking Punk to Power, Eliot Borenstein

Memory Politics and the Russian Civil War: Reds Versus Whites, Marlene Laruelle and Margarita Karnysheva

Russian Utopia: A Century of Revolutionary Possibilities, Mark D. Steinberg

Upcoming Titles

Art, History and the Making of Russian National Identity: Vasily Surkiov, Viktor Vasnetsov, and the Remaking of the Past, Stephen M. Norris

Russia and the Jewish Question: A Modern History, Robert Weinberg

The Soviet Gulag: History and Memory, Jeffrey S. Hardy

The Afterlife of the "Soviet Man": Rethinking Homo Sovieticus, Gulnaz Sharafutdinova

The Origins of Racism in Russia, Eugene M. Avrutin

The Multiethnic Soviet Union and its Demise, Brigid O'Keeffe

Russian Food since 1800: Empire at Table, Catriona Kelly

Meanwhile, In Russia: Russian Memes and Viral Video Culture, Eliot Borenstein

A Social History of the Russian Army, Roger R. Reese

Why We Need Russian Literature, Angela Brintlinger

RUSSIAN UTOPIA

A CENTURY OF REVOLUTIONARY POSSIBILITIES

Mark D. Steinberg

BLOOMSBURY ACADEMIC

LONDON • NEW YORK • OXFORD • NEW DELHI • SYDNEY

BLOOMSBURY ACADEMIC
Bloomsbury Publishing Plc
50 Bedford Square, London, WC1B 3DP, UK
1385 Broadway, New York, NY 10018, USA
29 Earlsfort Terrace, Dublin 2, Ireland

BLOOMSBURY, BLOOMSBURY ACADEMIC and the Diana logo are
trademarks of Bloomsbury Publishing Plc

First published in Great Britain 2021

Series design by Tjaša Krivec
Cover Image: Reproduction of Vladimir Tatlin's monument blueprints to
commemorate the Third International. The Collection of Moscow's Shchusev
Russian Architecture Museum (© SPUTNIK / Alamy Stock Photo)

A catalogue record for this book is available from the British Library.

A catalog record for this book is available from the Library of Congress.

ISBN: PB: 978-1-3501-2721-0
HB: 978-1-3501-2720-3
ePDF: 978-1-3501-2722-7
eBook: 978-1-3501-2719-7

Typeset by Deanta Global Publishing Services, Chennai, India

To find out more about our authors and books visit www.bloomsbury.com
and sign up for our newsletters.

CONTENTS

FIGURES

ACKNOWLEDGMENTS

I wrote this book during an unexpectedly historic time: amid the suffering, anxieties, and hopes of the year 2020. The quickly expanding coronavirus pandemic forced me to return home from research abroad and for many months kept me physically apart from friends and family, including from my son in New York City and my fiancée in northern Italy. But my situation was privileged compared, for example, to the millions of people "sheltering-in-place" in slums or without homes, the millions who lost jobs and incomes; the millions who lacked and still lack essential health care, sanitation, or even clean water; and the many hundreds of thousands who died. And yet, these troubled times, and the deep inequalities that made the impact of the pandemic so uneven, sparked rethinking about what had only recently seemed unchangeable. The novelist Arundhati Roy put it this way in early April, still the early days of what was becoming a global scourge:

> Historically, pandemics have forced humans to break with the past and imagine their world anew. This one is no different. It is a portal, a gateway between one world and the next. We can choose to walk through it, dragging the carcasses of our prejudice and hatred, our avarice, our data banks and dead ideas, our dead rivers and smoky skies behind us. Or we can walk through lightly, with little luggage, ready to imagine another world. And ready to fight for it.[1]

Such reimagining took an unexpected form also in response to the shock of yet another case of anti-Black police violence in the United States, the video-taped death of George Floyd, killed by a police officer kneeling on his neck on a Minneapolis street in late May. Massive demonstrations and scattered violence so terrified authorities that

Acknowledgments

the US president Donald Trump proclaimed these disturbances an "insurrection" that required military intervention to clear the streets,[2] and blamed protests on a "far-left fascism" that united "the Marxists, the anarchists, the agitators, the looters" to unleash disorder and "end America."[3] Many people recognized that race and poverty increased vulnerability to the coronavirus as well as to police violence. The mood on the streets was frustrated, angry, hopeful, and imaginative. We do not know where this will lead, if anywhere at all. We do know that out of the very darkness of tragedy arose some daring thinking about alternatives possibilities. A Black Lives Matter organizer, Nikita Mitchell, commented on this surprising new mood in late July: "As someone who has been in movement communities for a long time, it's deeply inspiring to me to see this level of analysis, dreaming, imagination. . . . We are on the cusp of something great, something historic. It keeps me going when I'm tired."[4]

Roy and Mitchell are both identifying a "utopian" moment in the sense of utopia used in this book: not as "nowhere," but as "not yet." Instead of the traditional definition of utopia as vain fantasies of perfection, this is utopia as a radical rethinking of possibility, as a critical method, as a productive disruption of assumptions.[5] These times, along with earlier encounters in my life with troubles and possibilities—social, political, personal—have shaped this book.

More immediately and concretely, I want to recognize the many individuals and groups who inspired this book and commented on my ideas and writing. I have been privileged to have been part of a remarkable academic community at the University of Illinois for the past twenty-five years: especially in the Department of History; the Department of Slavic Languages and Literatures; the Russian, East European, and Eurasian Center; the Humanities Research Institute; and the Unit for Criticism and Interpretive Theory. Conversations with Antoinette Burton, a brilliant colleague, whose intellectual perspectives have shaped so many of these programs, opened the door for this project, when she established the Center for Historical Interpretation, as part of which I would later lead a program around the theme of "Global Utopias." Much of my thinking about utopia was shaped in conversation with the many participants in this three-year project.

The faculty and graduate students in the interdisciplinary Russian Studies Circle ("the Kruzhok") have been a source of sustained critical conversations about Russian history and culture. I want to acknowledge especially key faculty colleagues in Russian and East European studies for their leadership as well as their engaged critical minds: Diane Koenker, John Randolph, Maria Todorova, Eugene Avrutin (coeditor of *Russian Shorts*), Harriet Murav, Valeria Sobol, Lilya Kaganovsky, David Cooper, Donna Buchanan, Kristin Romberg, and Carol Leff. And beyond Russian and East European studies, I am especially grateful to Antoinette Burton, Tamara Chaplin, Peter Fritzsche, Harry Liebersohn, Erik McDuffie, Kathryn Oberdeck, and Dorothee Schneider—from whom I have learned much and by whom I have been pushed to think harder. Not least, I want to thank the many students, undergraduate and graduate students, who in years of courses, conversations, and writings have made me think about what matters in history, how to interpret the past, and why I do this work.

Parts of this project were presented at the University of Illinois, the University of Turin, and at the European University Institute in Fiesole, Italy. I am grateful for the stimulating critical comments and questions. For their generosity in critically reading the entire manuscript, I am enormously grateful to Harriet Murav, John Randolph, Daniela Steila, and Maria Todorova. This book would not have been written without the initiative of Stephen Norris and Eugene Avrutin, who established the *Russian Shorts* series; Rhodri Mogford, the talented history publisher at Bloomsbury Academic; and the anonymous reviewers of my proposal and of the completed draft. Steve and Gene also provided essential critical readings of the proposal and the manuscript at different stages.

Finally, on a personal note, I want to dedicate this book to my son, Sasha Steinberg, and my partner, Daniela Steila. They have in so many powerful ways influenced my thinking about past and present and possibility. Sasha is not only an extraordinary drag queen and artist (Sasha Velour) but a true intellectual, cultural critic, and historian

Acknowledgments

who has encouraged me to think in many new ways, along with Sasha's partner, John Jacob Lee (Johnny Velour), and so many of the people in their New York drag world, who have welcomed me as Papa Velour (a title I cherish more than Professor Steinberg). They have all inspired and sustained me in some dark times. Daniela is not only a specialist on most of the writers and ideas I discuss but a personal miracle, a sign that the improbable is always possible.

INTRODUCTION

The ocean of possibility is much greater than our customary land of reality.

—Ernst Bloch, 1964

Soyez réalistes, demandez l'impossible (Be realistic, demand the impossible).

—slogan in Paris, May 1968

This book is about stories and dreams. They unfolded in a particular time and place—Russia from the eighteenth century into the twentieth. But good stories reach beyond time and place. Like folktales, they have a "moral." They take their cues from the "real world," the world as it is, in order to speak of what is not yet real, what is missing, what might lay beyond. Dreams interpret the world, but they also can change it. In sleep, dreams echo our fears and desires, transgress what everyday experience tells us is possible or not, imaginatively unleash our potential, and suspend disbelief. In dreams, it seems utterly realistic that people fly, become younger, or return from death, for these are our wishes. We can extend this to dreaming awake, which the German philosopher Ernst Bloch called "dreamwork" and "forward dreaming," and his colleague Walter Benjamin called "awakening" through "dream consciousness" to "truth." Dream consciousness sees beyond the horizon of what we can see in the present, toward the possible but not yet real. Sometimes, Bloch added, this forward vision may become "the dream that goes out to shape the external world." This is the utopian method.[1]

When I think about what "utopia" means, especially for the Russian stories I explore in this book, I look less to Thomas More, who coined the term in the sixteenth century, than to twentieth-century thinkers like Bloch and Benjamin.[2] Their experiences and dreams, experiments and traumas, speak to the modern Russian experience more strongly. And they speak more strongly to our own times, our own experiences of reality and possibility—the window through which we view the past. Bloch started each of his two great books on utopia in the midst of the devastating world wars of the last century. His view of these times was affected, no doubt, by his experiences as a Jew and a Marxist. Writing in, and about, the darkness of the world of the present, utopia was for Bloch not a hopeless fantasy about a nonexistent place or time (the literal "no-place" of "u-topia") but a critical method to question and transform reality. Not a "no-place" but a "not-yet."

The "utopian impulse," Bloch argued, is not about a place but a perception, an orientation, a method. And however future-oriented, utopia's real attention is on the present: "consciousness *wants* to look far into the distance"—geographically as More did to his imagined distant island or temporally as science fiction does to utopias set in the future—"but ultimately only in order to penetrate the darkness so near," to "venture beyond" the "darkness of the lived moment" in order to discover the "not-yet-become."[3] This perception is the "resonant energy of utopia."[4] After fleeing fascist Europe for the United States, Bloch documented this utopian impulse across histories of human practice: fairytales, music and dance, travel, leisure, fashion, architecture, philosophy, religion, morality, science, invention, literature, and "the dream-factory" of cinema. During the First World War, Bloch had described this consciousness in the lyrical language of dreams: as a "utopian impulse" to "summon what is not, build into the blue, build ourselves into the blue, and seek there the real, the true, where the merely factual disappears."[5] Many years later, in a conversation in the 1960s, he summarized utopian consciousness as the vague but nagging sense that "something's missing" in the world as it is and the awareness that we need not accept this lack as inevitable or eternal.[6]

In a variation on the Marxist metaphor of revolution as a "leap from the kingdom of necessity to the kingdom of freedom,"[7] Benjamin defined this utopian challenge to what we think to be the boundaries of reality and possibility as a revolutionary "leap in the open air of history," when humanity tries to "blast open the continuum of history" and grasp the "splinters of messianic time."[8] This is utopia as open-ended and unpredictable disruption of the now, looking toward possibility, not a closed map or blueprint of an impossible future. This is history not as gradual and linear progress toward a better life or the inevitable working out of some universal divine or rational plan but utopia as a leap into uncertainty, contingency, and chance, where there are no guarantees but an ocean of possibilities. At its most thoroughgoing, and most disruptive, this is utopia as critique of its own self, its claims to have built, especially from positions of power, something good and finished. This is utopia as knowing that in every accomplishment something is always missing, always unfinished, and yet not losing hope.

The dozens of people whose stories and dreams appear in this book would be nodding in agreement with these ideas, but they would vehemently protest my calling them "utopians." For most of them, utopia meant fanciful wish having nothing to do with reality. For socialists, in particular, to be called "utopian" was an insult. When Karl Marx wrote *Socialism: Utopian and Scientific*, he mocked the idealistic folly of the "utopians" for imagining that "truth, reason, and justice" would come to their world through the simple power of the human mind, through the workings of reason and morality. Historians of Russia have often used the label in the same way, frequently adding a greater accusation when writing about the Communist era: that Russia's revolutionary utopians so believed in their impossible dream of a perfected society and universal happiness, and in the "scientific" certainty that they understood the workings of history, and that they tried, with terrible and tragic consequences, to force their vision upon people's lives, revealing the nightmare lurking in the dream. But there are also historians who have recognized the complexity and varieties of utopian thinking in Russia, documented its everyday practices, recognized its critical spirit, and, most importantly, tried to understand people of the past as they understood themselves rather than dismiss their ideals and actions as naïve or insincere. This book is indebted to that tradition and continuing work.[9]

This is not to say that the people whose stories I consider did not succumb to fanciful desire and wishful illusion. Nor, to look fully into the darkness they could produce, is this to say that utopians did not do great harm when they acted with power in their hands and faith in their heads. Most of us prefer to celebrate those who dreamed and fought for "liberty, equality, and fraternity." But we must not ignore the brutalities that idealists could unleash, all too often in the name of people's happiness. Neither should we forget the harshness and brutalities of the world they hoped to change: the wounds of inequality, the intellectual and moral "darkness" of the majority of the population, the abuses of power, and the ubiquity of cruelty and violence. Russians were not at all unique in suffering from such conditions. Nor were their dreams of change directed only at curing Russia. Still, we should not dismiss the judgments of so many of them that Russian history and lives were darker than in the West: Russian rulers more cynical and arbitrary, Russia's poverty and ignorance deeper, Russian hatreds crueler, and Russian immoralities more appalling. And perhaps, too, they felt, Russian desires and visions of possibility were more intense and urgent.

It has been argued that every utopia "comes with its implied dystopia." The usual view of dystopia is the tendency, perhaps inevitability, for utopias to corrupt themselves in practice, especially in power. This is surely part of the story. But there is a deeper way to understand the relation between utopia and dystopia—not as a simple opposition but as a complex interrelationship: as the perceived dystopia of harsh reality, the "dystopia of the status quo," which inspires and shapes the utopian imagination.[10] This is dystopia not as the dark outcome of "utopia in power" but the darkness, especially in lived human experience, that utopia wants to negate. Intolerable conditions in the here and now nurture utopia's horizon of possibilities, its counter-ideals, its dreams. This is dystopia not as utopia's Other but its necessary twin: its inspiration as well as its dark potential.

As a volume in the *Russian Shorts* series, brevity means choices. I will not offer a comprehensive history that would be necessarily superficial and sketchy. I focus on a selection of individuals, whose stories and perspectives are *telling* of larger patterns and trends, but also distinct. I prefer to sacrifice breadth and the illusion of typicality in order to capture more of the depth and complexity of human experience, vision, and practice.

Across a century and a half, from the Enlightenment-inspired idealism of the eighteenth century to the Communist experiments, crises, and conflicts of the twentieth century, I explore utopian consciousness and practice among cultural elites and laboring commoners, in the halls of power and on the streets of resistance. We meet state leaders and revolutionaries; writers and artists; aristocrats and workers; socialists, anarchists, liberals, populists, and monarchists; Christians, Jews, and atheists; men and women; heterosexuals and homosexuals. I have organized the book thematically in order to highlight common questions and sometimes surprising connections, including to the world outside of Russia. Individual chapters tend to proceed chronologically, though each opens with a story from any point in that history that suggests much beyond itself. Chapter 1, "Wings of Utopia," explores the history of visual, literary, sacred, and practical obsessions with wings and human flight as transcendent possibility. Chapter 2, "The New Person," looks at how people imagined and tried to create the "new man" and the "new woman." Questions of morality, human dignity, self, community, freedom, and love are leitmotifs. Chapter 3, "The New City," looks at how modernizing cities were experienced as destructive, debasing, and ruinous, as dystopian, and at efforts to imagine and create cities that would be redemptive and liberating, social spaces for making a "modernity" that would enable people to overcome human backwardness and the limitations of the natural world through development, engineering, science, and "cultural revolution." In Chapter 4, "The New State," questions of freedom, justice, and happiness are key themes in how people, both rulers and dissenters, imagined and practiced political possibility.

In the Russian Empire and the USSR, the modern experience has been often harsh and painful, full of hopes and disappointments, dreams and tragedies. If we look at this history through the lens of utopia, we discover new perspectives on Russian history, and on the world history, of efforts to imagine and realize a transformed new life. *Russian Utopia* is a history of "the pursuit of happiness," which for many Russians meant liberty, justice, morality, community, and the dignity of the individual—ideals that stereotypes about Russian political culture might lead us to discount. And through it all we see a striking refusal to accept that the present is ever enough.

A final word about our own time and place. History writing is always partly a history of the present. Not because history repeats itself but because human lives share so much across boundaries of space and time, not least in how people understand wrong and right. By focusing on individual experiences and voices—listening in as people tried to make sense of, and question, their own difficult present with values, ideas, and emotions they found useful—*Russian Utopia* speaks also of troubles, uncertainties, dreams of possibility, and struggles in other times and places, including our own. "Incipit vita nova"—"here begins a new life"—is the phrase, from Dante, with which Bloch concluded the introduction to his 1918 book *Spirit of Utopia.* With these words he summoned a long history of desire and effort, which speaks at once of the studied past, the lived present, and possible futures. I hope to offer in this book something of the same.

CHAPTER 1
WINGS OF UTOPIA

An enemy of the spirit of gravity . . . he will one day teach Man to
fly . . . . As for the man who has not yet learned to fly, earth and
life seem grave.

—Friedrich Nietzsche, *Thus Spoke Zarathustra*, 1883–5

Anniversaries of historical events are times when we look to the past
to interpret the present and imagine the future, to think about who
we are. This is especially true of big, round numbers: a centenary or
bicentenary. No less interesting and revealing are first anniversaries:
the first time people mark an event as historical and try to define its
meanings and significance, especially *as* history. This was certainly
the case at the first anniversary of the October 1917 Revolution.[1]
Consider the situation and moods at that moment. Many Russians
believed that they were starting, in the midst of the catastrophe
of war, a global wave of revolutions that would change the world
forever, even, to quote from resolutions by radicalized soldiers in
the first days after October, an apocalyptic "final battle" against the
old world, the "long-awaited Great hour . . . for the realization of the
Great slogan of Liberty, Equality, and Fraternity."[2] Opponents of the
new Soviet government were no less hyperbolic as they condemned
the Bolsheviks for bringing suffering and destruction to the nation, "a
new stage on [Russia's] path of thorns."[3] In truth, so much remained
uncertain and vulnerable. Russia's war-torn economy was in shambles.
Civil war loomed across the collapsed empire. And the "public mood,"
journalists reported (until the independent press was silenced in the
midsummer of 1918), was "anxious," "confused," "depressed," and
"frightened."[4] This first anniversary was steeped in both desire and
anxiety. A time for explanation and imagination.

In preparation for the first anniversary celebrations in Moscow, recently made the new Soviet capital, the city sponsored a design competition for a memorial plaque to be installed on the Senate Tower of the Kremlin, facing Red Square, overlooking the graves of those who died fighting to establish the power of the soviets, the workers' and soldiers' councils in whose name the Bolshevik had seized state power. On the day of the festival, Red Square was filled with delegates from factories, the army, and neighborhood soviets. On the podium, beneath the veiled memorial, stood the leaders of the new Soviet state and the Bolshevik party, including Vladimir Lenin, the head of both party and state, who gave the main speech. As the curtain covering the memorial plaque was pulled down, the assembled crowd saw the work that won the competition, by Sergei Konenkov, a prominent revolutionary sculptor. To the music of a soldiers' orchestra and the voices of a workers' choir singing a "Cantata" specially written for the occasion, people saw a large, brightly colored bas-relief, dominated by a bare-chested golden-skinned figure, with huge white wings, clad in a classical skirt, wearing a crown of eagle feathers. This female figure— female according to the artist, though visually androgynous—holds a palm branch in one hand (modestly covering her chest) and a flowing red banner in the other. Behind her, the rays of the rising sun form the words "October 1917 Revolution." Broken swords and discarded guns wrapped in mourning bands are stuck into the ground along with two fallen red flags. On one of these flags are inscribed the golden words, "To the Fallen in the Struggle for Peace and the Brotherhood of Peoples." The choir sang "Come down from the cross, crucified people / And be transformed . . . / Roar, land, with the final storm . . . / Let a new day shine in the azure, / The old world transfigured"[5] (see Figure 1).

Looking back a century later, we might be surprised that such imagery would be chosen by a communist state to express their vision of the revolution, and to mark such an exceptionally significant place and time: the central revolutionary necropolis (later the bodies of Lenin and other leading revolutionaries would be buried or displayed there, with festive marches regularly parading past) on the very first

Figure 1 Sergei Konenkov, "To the Fallen in the Struggle for Peace and the Brotherhood of Peoples," Memorial bas-relief plaque, 1918. © Photograph in Mikhail Guerman, *Art of the October Revolution* (Leningrad: Avrora, 1979).

anniversary celebration of the revolution. Death and memory, power and possibility, entwined at this moment. And the memorial plaque suggested something of the sacred about it all. When Konenkov was installing his memorial on the Kremlin tower, an old woman approached and asked the bearded sculptor, "Hey, *batiushka* [father, a name also used for priests], to whom are they putting up this icon?" He answered, "Revolution." To which she responded: "it's the first time I have heard of that saint."[6] Whether the old woman was sarcastic or innocently confused, her visual expectation of the sacred is understandable.

The imagery was eclectic and global in its allusions to the sacred—the rising sun (the dawning age of light against the darkness of the past), the female personification of the revolution (echoing the figure of Liberty made popular by the French Revolution, reaching back to the Roman Libertas), the palm branch (a familiar symbol of martyrdom, victory, and heaven), and red banners (symbol of revolution and socialism, but also of the blood of the fallen). And then there were the themes of crucifixion, resurrection, and new life in the proletarian cantata.

But I want us to think about the wings. Other approved public art for the first anniversary, including the runner-up proposal for the Red Square memorial,[7] featured winged figures, usually female, sometimes blowing trumpets.[8] Wings, and the power of the winged to fly, have been a cultural theme and symbol across centuries and cultures. Obvious influences on the image of winged Revolution include the Greco-Roman goddesses Nike/Victoria and, with wings and trumpet, Pheme/Fama; winged deities, many of them female, in the ancient cultures of Egypt, Persia, Asia, the Americas, and the Slavic world; the angels and archangels of the monotheistic religions (Zoroastrianism, Judaism, Christianity, Islam)—likely to be male but androgynous—with their promises of protection and salvation and the coming of "a new heaven and a new earth," notably the Archangels Michael and Gabriel, who foretell the coming of the Messiah and the final defeat of evil, proclaimed by Gabriel on his horn; Russian folk traditions, including mythic creatures such as the Firebird, the object of magical quests in Russian folklore, and Sirin, the half-woman "Heavenly Bird of Paradise" who sings songs of future happiness; and the modern revolutionary and socialist tradition of winged female figures, embodying ideals and virtues, often with a symbolic breast bared, and blowing trumpets.[9]

Beyond angels and allegories is human flight—a strong expression of the utopian impulse to venture beyond the limited world of the here and now. Men with crafted wings like Daedalus and Icarus (especially the son who refused to obey his father's warning not to fly too close to the sun), shamans and witches, the supermen of philosophy and comic books, and airplanes and spaceships are among many forms in which humans have expressed the dream of flight in imagination and practice. And, of course, there are our sleeping dreams. The desire to fly embodies the human determination to transcend the limits of reality; to venture beyond the grounded every day; to soar "into the blue" toward what is yet to be, as Ernst Bloch put it; to leap in "the open air of history," as Walter Benjamin put it.[10] Friedrich Nietzsche also comes to mind, and is worth recalling not only for his enormous influence on Russian intellectuals but for his specific impact on the artist Konenkov.[11] Nietzsche's famous Zarathustra declares himself "an enemy of the spirit of gravity" and prophesies that the superman will "one day teach Man to fly." Until then, Zarathustra warns, "the man who has not yet learned to fly" will feel that the "earth and life are grave," for this is the world as it is, rather than as it ought to be, and so as it will be.[12]

Working-class poets in Russia, lacking literary training, and writing in moments stolen from work or sleep,[13] often reached for images of flight and wings to describe radical transcendence of the world as it is. In memoirs, some workers recalled actual childhood desires to fly as a way out of their harsh lives.[14] One of very few women worker-poets whose work found its way into print, Maria Chernysheva prayed for wings of escape from the "shameful chains" of "slavery" in her 1910 poem: "Give me wings! Swift, light wings . . . / And I would revel in the freedom of flight" and soar "toward the open expanse."[15] Socialist workers believed such wings of freedom and transcendence would be found in class struggle. In Alexei Bibik's 1912 autobiographical novel of working-class life, *Toward the Open*

Road, when the worker-hero first experiences the power and freedom of a strike, he feels that "wings" have grown on his back.[16] In 1914, the president of the St. Petersburg Union of Metalworkers, Alexei Gastev, published a poem in the union's newspaper that culminated in this ringing declaration: "Higher still, yet higher! In the smoke of victory, we dash from the highest rocks, from the most treacherous cliffs to the most distant heights! / We have no wings? / We will! They will be born in an explosion of burning wish."[17] Other worker-writers imagined themselves as eagles or comets inspiring people with their flight.

Maxim Gorky, himself a largely self-taught writer who was much admired by worker-writers and the socialist left, often embodied revolutionary aspiration in winged flight: his "Song of the Storm Petrel" (1901) and "Song of the Falcon" (1902) presented the flights of the boldest of birds as images of soaring possibility, courage in the face of danger and death, and freedom. In 1903, his fantasy-poem "Humanity" (*Chelovek*) imagined human life as a psychological struggle among winged qualities: winged "Thought," humanity's strongest ally and friend, against winged Melancholy, Lies, Hatred, and Death.[18] In Gorky's 1908 novel *Confession*, the awakened people "fly over the earth irresistibly," overcoming doubts and fears, and performing miracles.[19]

In the atmosphere of fear and hope during the revolution and the civil war, worker-poets were even more likely to use images of wings and flight. In May 1917, for example, the Socialist Revolutionary newspaper *The People's Cause* published a poem by Pyotr Oreshin about the experience of peasant revolution: "Across fields I'm flying / On the fiery wings of time."[20] A year later, Oreshin imagined creatures with "golden wings" appearing out of heaven and hell to fly Russia into a new age free of suffering.[21] In 1919, the working-class Bolshevik poet Vasily Alexandrovsky read at numerous public meetings a poem simply titled "Wings," in which the bloodshed of war and revolution is overcome when flowing blood turns to empowering lava and everyone grows wings to survive and transcend the rivers of blood.[22] Other images were more heroic, even promethean, as in Ilya Sadofev's declaration: "We are winged aspiration. / We are omnipotent and can do as we wish, / Destroy, achieve."[23] Very often, these revolutionary wings were made not of ordinary feathers but of iron, gold, and especially fire. Indeed, "fire-winged" became a widely used post-October adjective for describing the revolution, including "fire-winged factories," "fire-winged ideas," and, we have seen, "the fiery wings of time."[24]

Revolutionary wings and human flight were often linked to resurrection. Mikhail Gerasimov—a former railway worker, a leader of the Proletcult (the "proletarian culture" movement), and one of the authors of the "Cantata" sung over the graves of the dead of October at the dedication of Konenkov's memorial—published a poem called "We Are Flying" in a 1918 Proletcult collection, *Fire-Winged Factory*, which envisions a worker's deliverance from the deadening life in the factory as resurrection and flight to the sun. As the poem continues, this resurrecting flight "into the unreachable sky" becomes both more modern and more cosmic: flying is propeller-powered, on wings made of iron, and the space won is that of the sun and stars.[25] Gerasimov's vision echoed a whole world of Russian "cosmist" thought about a future when science and technology would overcome death, resurrect the dead of the past, and colonize the universe and beyond to make room for immortal humanity.[26]

Space flight to utopia—a variation on the theme of journeys to utopias across uncharted seas or across time—was a tradition reaching back at least to Francis Godwin's early seventeenth-century tale, *The Man in the Moon*. In Russia, the influential Bolshevik activist and writer Alexander Bogdanov blended new scientific and technical knowledge, traditions of utopian fiction and science fiction, widespread fascination (scientific and fanciful) with Mars and Martians, and Marxist ideology into his 1908 novel, *Red Star*.[27] The story begins in the opening days of the 1905 revolution, a time of hope and expectation that gave way, by the time Bogdanov was writing, to what journalists described as moods of "demoralization," "cynicism," and "apathy."[28] In Bogdanov's novel, a revolutionary named Leonid is chosen by a delegation of Martians to fly back with them to the Red Planet in order to learn of their superior social order but also to teach them about earth, perhaps to become an emissary as they spread their ideals across the universe. To find the right person, the

Martians search among "all the major peoples of the world," but are disappointed by most people's values and vision. Russians are found to be the most suitable, however, because, given present realities, "more than anywhere else, people are forced to look to the future."[29] A Marxist is naturally the most future-oriented of Russians and hence the most suited for this mission to Mars. The Martian utopia is partly what a socialist reader at the time might have expected and admired: rational, stateless, collectivist, and egalitarian. Individuals are free in work, consumption, love, and sex. This is not because individual freedom is valued as a moral good. Rather, rationality rules and the only value is what is for the collective good. Indeed, this is a society regulated by statistics and technology, which suited progressive ideals at the time. Nature is an enemy to conquer. And there is a still darker side that Leonid discovers to his horror, indeed that drives him to madness and murder: the cold and scientific consideration of a plan to colonize earth that would require, rationally, the genocidal eradication of humans.

While the Martian utopia has attracted most attention, a large section of the book is about the flight. The journey is an opportunity for Leonid to learn about Martian ways. No less important, the flight is itself a transformative experience. The Martian spacecraft is an "etheroneph" made of "pure crystal," glass, steel, and precious metals, powered by anti-gravitational "minus matter" and nuclear fission. On the journey, he experiences weightlessness. "I could feel," Leonid writes, "my body becoming lighter and my movements freer."[30] Like Zarathustra's superman, Martians learned to overcome gravity and to "teach Man to fly." Once accustomed to the sensation, and no longer feeling nausea, Leonid revels in the pleasure: "we inhabitants of the etheroneph all became something like fantastic acrobats, able to fly without wings."[31]

Airplanes and aviators, and later rocket ships and cosmonauts, were leitmotifs in Soviet culture, symbols of progress and power, of technology and science overcoming backwardness and tradition.[32] Well before the 1917 revolution, Russians were fascinated by aviation—not only for its practical uses, particularly in war, but as an easy-to-read sign of the human power to overcome time and space and venture beyond the familiar into the new and unknown. Scientists like Konstantin Tsiolkovsky, a pioneer of aeronautics and rocket science, worked on projects for space flight as part of a vision of a future humanity spread throughout the cosmos. In Communist Russia, the fascination with air flight grew into a cult. Actual religion was an enemy, of course, and flight could serve this cause. Famously, even somewhat comically, early Soviet activists promoting "godlessness" invited peasants to take airplane flights to see that there is no God in the heavens, with pilots declaring they had performed "air baptisms" of converted peasants.[33] Many years later, the Soviet Union's famous cosmonaut Yuri Gagarin (memorialized in a giant Moscow monument as a titanium superman flying into space, without a rocket ship) was famously (and probably falsely) said to have declared that in the beauty of space he saw "no god." In political propaganda, especially in Stalin's time, airplanes and pilots were a major theme—as in the 1935 poster, "Long Live Our Happy Socialist Motherland," where airplanes named for Lenin, Stalin, Gorky, and other Soviet notables fly over the masses on Red Square (see Figure 2). By the way, just behind Stalin, who stands on Lenin's mausoleum, though out of our sight, was Konenkov's 1918 winged angel of revolution, which remained on the Kremlin Wall facing Red Square until the 1940s.[34]

   Russian and Soviet artists and architects, like so many philosophers and scientists, turned often to flight for its power to represent human desire and the human capacity to leap beyond the limitations of the world as given. We could explore many examples of flying men and women in art and design. We might look at Natalia Goncharova's *Mystical Images of War* (1914), in which both airplanes and angels soar above struggling armies and citizens. Or at the paintings of Kazimir Malevich, such as his *Aviator* (1914) and *Suprematist Composition: Airplane Flying* (1915), or of Marc Chagall, who continually returned to lovers and angels, as in *Over the Town* (1918) and the many blue angels he painted in emigration after 1923. In the 1920s, the artist Anton Lavinsky proposed a "city in the air" made of glass and asbestos and resting on springs, which, a sympathetic critic explained, would bring liberation and lightness, not as an immediately buildable plan but as a challenge to human perceptions of possibility.[35] Vladimir Tatlin

Figure 2 Gustav Klutsis, "Long Live Our Happy Socialist Motherland, Long Live Our Beloved Great STALIN!" 1935 Poster. © Public Domain.

constructed "Letatlin" (1929–32), in which his family name and the Russian word "to fly" titled a set of crafted wings for human flight. In 1928, the architect Georgy Krutikov presented a project for the "City of the Future," where workers live in floating buildings far above the earth and fly to earthbound industrial and cultural zones in personal rockets that also worked as submarines and automobiles (see Chapter 3). "Avia-march" was one of the most popular Soviet songs of the 1930s: "We are born to make fairy-tales into reality, / To conquer time and space. / Our reason gave us steel arms—wings, / and instead of a heart, a flaming motor. / Ever higher, higher, and higher . . ." I could go on with many more examples. It is not surprising that when the American journalist Eugene Lyons, who reported from Moscow in the late 1920s and early 1930s, described his growing disillusionment with Soviet socialism, in a book he titled *Assignment in Utopia*, he reached for the unavoidable metaphor of wings: "The Russian revolution gave wings to earthbound hopes. My problem, the moral and intellectual problem of millions who know that the revolution has been betrayed and perverted, was to disown the perversions without clipping those wings."[36]

Of these and other possible examples of utopian visions of flight, I will pause over the work of the famous Soviet poet and playwright Vladimir Mayakovsky. During the First World War, in his long poem "Man" (*Chelovek*, or Person), Mayakovsky imagined a symbolic version of himself flying into the cosmos to flee the darkness of the lived present, a world of necessity not freedom. This present darkness is not so much the immediate brutality of wartime death and destruction but the deeper and systemic violence of a society where money rules. Money—despised and rejected in so many utopias, including Thomas More's original—is the antithesis of life, feelings, thought, and poetry; it is the heart of darkness, says Mayakovsky. The "Man" in this poem is a poet who happens to be named "Mayakovsky." He dreams of another possible life. But unable to change the debased world, he decides that suicide is the only way out. With that thought, his body rises into the air and disappears into space, a flight visible to people on the streets who cry out in astonishment. He reaches heaven, a cloudland of "cleansed smoothness" where everything "is in frightfully good order." He finds this to be a rather melancholy utopia without life, emotion, thinking, or time. No need for poetry there, either. After thousands of earth years, for time has no meaning in heaven, "Mayakovsky" returns to earth, only to find that nothing has changed. Heaven and earth, space and time, once again disappoint, leaving him adrift in the vast nowhere of space—the emptiest sort of "utopia."[37]

Revolution, which seemed so unlikely in 1916, came at the beginning of 1917. For Mayakovsky, as for so many, it was a redemptive miracle that transformed time and space, the whole of history past and future, and the entire cosmos: "Today, the thousand-year-old 'Before' has collapsed. / Today, the foundation of worlds has been reconsidered . . .. / The paths of the planets, the power of existence, are subject to our will. / The land is ours. / The air is ours."[38] In 1925, Mayakovsky developed this picture of revolution embracing the sky and the cosmos into an explicitly utopian fantasy, "The Flying Proletarian." The poem opens in the year 2025 as America declares war against the USSR, which was a real fear in Russia in 1925. In defense, Soviet proletarians take to the air, chanting their heroic march: "We are the flyers / of the workers' and peasants' republic. / We are flying / with shining wings." Even the birds of the air are astonished by how high these proletarians fly. The American enemy, whose airplane wings are emblazoned with "KKK" and swastikas, are overwhelming and unstoppable. "The revolution is in danger," radios blare. Then suddenly, the enemy retreats: in New York City the proletariat has rebelled in solidarity, uniting America to the Soviet Union to create a global "commune without slaves or masters."

The poem then speculates on a post-revolutionary future, a new world built around human flight: "In Moscow / there will be / no lanes nor streets / just airport-homes." Citizens will work only a few hours a day thanks to electric automation—and at home enjoy automated toothbrushes and razors. The man of the future (and the emphasis is on men as defining mankind) flies to work in a dirigible. Many factories are in the air and even work with air, such as a factory making sour cream and milk from clouds. Children fly to school. Anti-religious education is somehow still needed in the twenty-first century, so students join their teacher on a flight into the heavens to see for themselves that there are "no gods, no angels." Private home kitchens have been replaced by communal "aero-dining halls" where the dishes wash themselves. Leisure, which is most of the day, might be a flight "with one's wife" to visit friends, a game of "avia-ball" (old-fashioned earthbound football is too boring for these flying proletarians), enjoying a "radio-book," watching cinema projected onto clouds, or going to a dance in the sky with flying tables where one might rest and have a drink (nonalcoholic, of course). When ready for bed, one can fold one's personal airplane and set it in a corner "like an umbrella." If such "winged days" of the future are to be made real, Mayakovsky concludes, if we are no longer to "crawl like a louse" in an earthbound life, we must "demand the sky." "Workers! / Peasants! / Check with your own hands / that / the heavens / are yours! / Demand the sky. / Thrust / the sharpened knife / of words / into the future that was not and is not."[39] The future that is "not-yet," we might translate these final words with Bloch's term.

Sex was often visible only around the edges or in the shadows of these stories of flight and future, for Marxist fantasies of flight kept their gaze on politics rather than personal life. Bogdanov's hero Leonid is criticized by an earthly comrade with whom he was intimate for his amoral and libertine views of love and sex. Indeed, Leonid finds the open relationships on Mars appealing. But these are minor themes, easily missed, and censored in some Soviet editions of the book. Even Mayakovsky, whose tumultuous love life was well known and found its way into his poetry, barely implied what love and sex might look like in a new society.

But a few writers recognized that the intimate was also a matter for history and politics. Alexandra Kollontai, a leader of the Women's Section of the Communist Party, published in 1923 an open letter to young people, "Make Way for Winged Eros." The time has come, she argued, to create a rich and flourishing sexual life such as is unknown in the bourgeois world or possible during the hard years of revolutionary struggle in Russia, something radically

> new. Now . . . when the atmosphere of revolutionary battles has ceased to completely consume the person, leaving nothing, tender-winged Eros, contemptuously cast aside for a time, has again begun to assert its rightful place . . . "Wingless Eros" no longer satisfies the needs of our spirits . . . . The many-stringed lyre of the lavishly winged god of love drowns the monotonous voice of "wingless Eros."

But this was still only the new love possible in the present, not yet a revolutionary leap into the open air of romantic and sensual possibility:

> In the realized communist society, love, "winged Eros," will appear in a different, transfigured form complete unknown to us . . . . Even the boldest fantasy is incapable of imagining what it will look like . . . . But it is clear that in place of the meager feathers on the wings of the Eros of the past, the ideology of the dawning class can cause to grow new feathers of beauty, strength, and brightness never seen before.[40]

Years before Kollontai embraced the metaphor of wings to imagine the liberated intimacy of the new person in the new world, Mikhail Kuzmin offered an even bolder vision, not limited to normative heterosexuality, in his 1906 novella *Wings*.[41] The utopian vision in *Wings* was not that of an imaginary place or time but that of the presence in the present, and continued emergence, of the people of the future, of the "new person" (*novyi chelovek*) "with wings." The novel's openly gay, elder theorist of the new, the English-Russian Larion Shtrup, tells the unsure young hero of the novel, Vanya Smurov, while they sit together on a bench in St. Petersburg's Summer Garden (in reality, a known cruising ground for gay men), that "you have within you, Vanya, the resources to become a genuine new person . . . a completely modern man if you want."[42] But this requires freeing oneself from the prejudiced norms of the world as it is, especially views of beauty, love, the body, and sex. The new and modern person, Shtrup argues, has a sense of beauty and pleasure that unites Eros and aesthetics, that recovers and modernizes forgotten classical values of beauty, sexual freedom, and what is "natural," in order to create from that lost past a radical future:

> We are Hellenes, lovers of the beautiful, bacchants of a future life . . . . There is our ancestral fatherland, flooded in sunlight and freedom, with bold and beautiful people, and it is to that place, across the sea, through the fog and gloom, we are going, Argonauts! In a newness never before heard we recognize our

most ancient roots, and in a radiance never before seen we sense our fatherland.

In that land, the celebration of beauty knows no boundaries, neither sexual nor moral, and lust and love are never separate. It is a land with "the most blazing life, where every pleasure would be heightened as if you had only just been born and might die at any moment . . . . Miracles surround us at every step."[43]

Of course, the only way to reach that free and bright land of the future, which is also a vision of the distant past, is with wings. "People saw," Shtrup explains to friends while walking in the park, for he is continually discoursing on the subject, "that every sort of Beauty, every sort of love was from the gods, and they become free and bold, and they grew wings."[44] In the final pages of the story, after having fled Russia for Italy, Vanya has become more open to this liberated world of love and beauty and to his own homosexuality, which had disgusted and frightened him. Shtrup tells Vanya, "One more effort, and you will grow wings. I can already see them." To which Vanya admits, "Maybe, but it is very difficult while they are growing."[45] An Italian writer, Ugo Orsini, a close friend of Shtrup's, is writing a play on these themes, which he describes to the fascinated Vanya:

> Act III: on the blessed glades there are scenes from *Metamorphoses*, where gods take on every kind of form for love, where Icarus falls, Phaeton falls, and Ganymede [the beautiful youth abducted by an eagle for Zeus] says, "Poor brothers, only I remain of all of you who flew into the sky, because you were drawn toward the sun by pride and children's toys, whereas I was seized by raging love."[46]

Kollontai was harshly criticized by orthodox Communists for her arguments about "winged Eros." But her treatment was mild compared to the way Kuzmin was savaged by his contemporaries. If "winged Eros" frightened Orthodox Marxist moralists, homosexual love terrified people for whom same-sex intimacy was the ultimate transgression of traditional boundaries. *Wings* was condemned as "pornographic," "repulsive," and "nauseating," even though actual sexual relations are only very discreetly alluded to in the novel.[47]

Wings were for dreamers who believed that beyond the boundaries that history and society had established lies the open air of possibility and freedom. To recall Bloch's image of the utopian impulse in 1918, they were determined to "summon what is not" and seek "in the blue" a truth beyond the "merely factual" life of the world as it is, to recognize and bring into life the "not yet." But there were also always people, guardians of the status quo or simply people afraid to "fly," who echoed ancient worries about flying too high. The allegory of Icarus, whose wings melted in the sun's heat, was a warning to the boldest dreamers. But as the rest of this book considers, around questions about the "new person," the "new city," and the "new state," the Icarian spirit persisted as did its critics.

CHAPTER 2
THE NEW PERSON

. . . awakening in the people of a sense of their human dignity, lost in the mud and filth for so many centuries.

—Vissarion Belinsky, 1847

You may say that I'm a dreamer [*fantazerka*] . . .
—Vera Pavlovna in Chernyshevsky's *What Is to Be Done?* (1862)

Words carry histories, often lost in translation. *Chelovek* is one of these. It has been translated as person, human being, or man (though the Russian is gender-neutral).[1] But as the word worked through Russia's history, it became laden with ideas about the nature of the human being, especially human "qualities" of reason, free will, moral understanding, and conscience, and, inevitably, with ideas about human dignity and rights.[2] Significantly, it was linked to another elusive Russian word: *lichnost'*—person, personality, self, and individual, the essence of a person's humanity. The emerging ideal of the "*new* person," with its own multifaceted global history from antiquity to communism, complicated these meanings all the more.

This brings us to one of the most influential books ever written in Russia, Nikolai Chernyshevsky's novel, *What Is to Be Done? Stories about New People*. Like many Russian intellectuals of the eighteenth and nineteenth centuries, Chernyshevsky was many things: biographical dictionaries describe him as a philosopher, theoretician, scholar, literary critic, journalist, editor, writer, and revolutionary. He wrote *What Is to Be Done?* while in prison awaiting trial for political subversion. After its publication in 1863—that it was approved by the censors has been explained as "spectacular bureaucratic bungling"[3]— its influence was enormous. It was part of a sort of political debate of novels: it was a critical response to Ivan Turgenev's recent novel of ideas, *Fathers and Sons*, and was answered in turn by Fyodor Dostoevsky's *Notes from the Underground*. But its influence was deeper and immediate. Readers embraced its "new people" and their new morality as models for a socially conscious and transformed new life. Forty years later, the prominent Marxist Georgy Plekhanov still felt the influence and power of the book.

> Who has not read and reread this famous work? . . . Who has not become cleaner, better, braver, and bolder under its good influence? Who has not been struck by the moral purity of its main characters . . . . We have all drawn moral strength and faith in a better future from it.[4]

Vladimir Lenin recalled that under its influence "hundreds of people became revolutionaries," including himself. Shortly after the future Lenin turned seventeen, his older brother was executed for participating in a political conspiracy to assassinate Alexander III. "Knowing that Chernyshevsky's novel was one of his favorite books," Lenin wrote, he took the book from his brother's shelves and carefully read it over the course of a week to understand his sacrifice. "It is a thing that supplies energy for a whole lifetime," he concluded.[5] Lenin would later title his own defining book on how to make a revolution in Russia *What Is to Be Done?* The book touched readers in almost a spiritual way. Indeed, the book has been called "a new Gospel," its story of the transfiguration of all life part of a long tradition of translating sacred visions into secular utopias.[6]

It was also very much a book of its time. The novel's main character, Vera Pavlovna (the Russian word *vera* means "faith"), escapes her comfortable but oppressive family home and potentially disastrous fiancé by marrying her brother's tutor, a progressive young medical student named Dmitry Lopukhov. They tell each other they have fallen in love: she with him because he did not consider her "immoral" for admitting her secret wish, shared with most women, to be treated by her husband the way he treats strangers, with deference and respect; he with her for asking, "is it really possible to arrange things so that people can live happily."[7] They organize their life together in this spirit: each with a room of their own, which the other may enter only with permission, and a shared common room. To ensure her own economic independence, but also to act for the social good—key values for the new people—Vera establishes a small seamstress shop, which she turns into a cooperative, sharing the profits and organizing a commune for her workers. When Vera Pavlovna finds greater love with their best friend (another medical student, Kirsanov), Lopukhov accepts this. To free her, divorce being almost impossible at the time, he feigns suicide. In fact, he goes to America and builds a new identity. He eventually returns, marries, and the two couples live together in harmony in a communal apartment.

Along the way, Vera encounters other significant characters, notably the "extraordinary person," Rakhmetov, who gives away his wealth, takes up hard manual labor, and sleeps on a bed of nails to test and fortify himself. He too disappears to America, and the way people talk of his hoped-for return is as of Christ's Second Coming. Chernyshevsky tells the reader why he has introduced Rakhmetov to the novel even though he appears late and plays little part in the plot: to show that "new people" like Vera Pavlovna, Lopukhov, and Kirsanov are "simple, ordinary people." They may seem to us, to the society of the present, to be "soaring above the clouds." But that is only because we are "sitting in some godforsaken underworld." But they are there, just as a "bouquet is within fine wine. They are its strength and its aroma . . . the salt of the salt of the earth." They are the harbingers of a future we cannot even imagine.[8] The novel ends with poetic allusions to a coming revolution that will transform the world: "black fear," "darkness and cold," and "the odor of decay" are dispelled by "light, warmth, and aroma . . . the fragrance of roses." But, like fully realized new people, that is still in the future.[9]

Dreams play an essential role in the narrative. Most of the novel's "actions" are long talks about ideas: about the individual and society, friendship and love, oppression and freedom, hierarchy and equality. But key moments in Vera's growing consciousness of these values, and the inspiration for key decisions in her life, take place in dreams. Reasoning alone, it seems, is not enough for her to leap into the open air of the new. Dreams disrupt reality, transforming what experience tells us are the limits of the real into the realm of extraordinary possibility.[10]

In Vera's first dream, she is "locked up in a damp, dark cellar," when suddenly a door opens and she finds herself "running and frolicking" in an open field that she had not known existed. She then realizes she had been born paralyzed and had not known that "others can walk and run" until she is leaping in the field. She meets the one who has cured and freed her: a universal "bride" and "sister" who calls herself "love for humanity."[11] After this dream, she starts talking about her family home as a "cellar," now realizing that she was living in a "godforsaken underworld," and seeking the open air of freedom that she did not know was even possible.

Her second dream opens with a tedious discussion among men— throughout the book, in fact, men show little willingness to welcome women into their philosophical discussions—about the health or sickness of soil and the necessity of human activity and labor to ensure healthy nature. Various individuals, mostly from Vera's life but also from the street, confess to Vera their own filthy natures. Then, "love for humanity" reappears and reminds Vera that evil is necessary for good to grow, but in the future "when the good are strong, I will not need the wicked."[12] After this dream, Vera Pavlovna establishes her workshop as a cooperative—a project carried forward on "the wings of daydreams."[13]

The late Italian soprano Angiolina Bosio—whose performances in Russia in the 1850s of Verdi's new opera *La Traviata* (a tragic story of a "fallen woman" seeking freedom and love) made her hugely popular— appears in Vera Pavlovna's third dream, insisting that Vera read aloud from a private diary that Vera had not written in real life and in which words appear at Bosio's ghostly touch. Vera admits in the diary that it is not her husband she truly loves but "her deliverance from the cellar." As her liberator, Lopukhov deserves "gratitude and devotion, but only that." When they make love "his blood seethes and his caresses burn," but her desire is for "quiet, long caresses and to doze blissfully in a sea of tenderness."[14]

Vera Pavlovna's fourth dream offers the revelatory climax of her growing consciousness of what a new life and new people might be like, and an answer to the question "what is to be done?" Echoing previous dreams, the dream opens with a beautiful woman singing in a bright and fragrant field. The source of the voice appears, a "radiant beauty," uncannily familiar yet not seen before. She tells Vera that "none of you yet knows me in all my beauty." She becomes Vera's guide, promising to reveal "what was, what is, and what shall be." "They fly" to the first scene, a world of love, sensuality, and indolent bliss ruled by the fertility goddess Astarte. But as women in that world are servile and subordinate slaves, Vera's guide explains that there is no place for her there. A second scene appears: a magnificent city, filled with wealth and pleasure, where they worship Aphrodite, the goddess of love, beauty, and sexuality. But the "radiant beauty" tells Vera that this only appears to be a "kingdom of love," but "I did not exist then. They bowed down before the woman, but they did not consider her an equal. They worshipped her, but only as a source of pleasure. They did not acknowledge her human dignity . . . . They had no freedom. . . . Where there is no freedom, there is no happiness, and I do not exist." A new scene appears, a world of knights, castles, crusades, and chivalry, where the woman is worshipped but not touched. Their goddess is Chastity, the Virgin Mary, "modest, gentle, tender" and more beautiful than Astarte or Aphrodite, but full of sorrow. This virginal goddess says, "My soul is sad unto deathly sorrow. A sword has pierced my heart. You must grieve as well . . . . The earth is a vale of tears." The "radiant beauty" says, "No, no, I did not exist then."

These past worlds are present still, Vera is told, though they are fading as women are "awakened" to the truth "that she too is a human being [*chelovek*]." The "radiant beauty" manifests the future and reveals herself to Vera, who recognizes "her own self, but as a goddess." The goddess explains, "There is nothing nobler than a human being, nothing nobler than a woman. I am each woman to whom I appear." Like Christ, she is a god who becomes human to show people that they can become gods. She combines and magnifies the best qualities of all the goddesses before her—sensuality, beauty, "reverence before purity"—but also new qualities, especially equality, equal rights, human dignity, and freedom.

She then shows Vera the future. After a great rupture, the new world is born. Its architecture and household design are bright and open, made of crystal, glass, and aluminum. Labor in factories has been replaced by the work of automated machines. People still labor in the fields, to be in nature and sing in the sunshine. Everyone is exceptionally healthy, almost eternally young. Deserts have become lands of "milk and honey." Everyone is free to live as they choose, though most people choose to live as others do for this is rational and beneficial—this is the kingdom of freedom but also the kingdom of heaven. Evenings are filled with music and dance and "the full ecstasy of pleasure." This future is "many generations" away. It is still only a dream. But it is also dream consciousness, which awakens and inspires forward-looking action. The goddess's elder sister, who appeared in Vera's first dream with the name "love for humanity," tells Vera what is to be done: "Bring as much as you can from the future into the present."

More than fifty years later, "Natasha's Dreams: A Story" appeared in the Bolshevik journal for women, *Woman Worker* (*Rabotnitsa*). The author, Praskovia Kudelli, was one of the most prominent Bolshevik women. Echoing Vera Pavlovna's story in a proletarian key, Natasha has been fired from her job as a seamstress because she is judged a troublemaker. Returning to her rented corner, full of melancholy thoughts about where and what is "happiness," she falls asleep and sees "a beautiful young woman, a miraculous beauty" with flowers in her hair who offers to answer her question by showing her life in three dreams. In the first dream, Natasha is living an idle and luxurious existence, richly ornamented with jewels, but at a price: to be the mistress of a disrespectful and debauched man who cruelly reminds her that "I bought you" with all this luxury and so "you are mine." A normal girl would be grateful for such "happiness," he declares. Natasha rejects being a "bought woman." In her second dream, she is a worker in a large textile factory, a "cruel and cold" place into which men and women go through gates that remind her of the "jaws of a monster devouring its victims." The first victims to fall are the children, unwatched, living on the streets. Her own son, she learns, has died. In her lament she asks, "Why do our children perish! Why do they suffer?

Why do we suffer? We work ceaselessly, earning our crust of bread by the sweat of our brow! We live honestly! It so is so hard! Where is truth and justice?" (The word she uses, *Pravda*, suggests both ideas.) The miraculous beauty appears, embraces her, and promises to show her the path toward happiness and truth and justice. Into the air they fly to a "great city." Looking through a window, Natasha is shown men and women who are happy, though the present remains dark, for they know that the future world of brotherhood and equality, "when people will be people, not beasts," is "inevitable," a "law of life." Those "who bring the new life closer" are "happy," the beautiful woman tells her. Even in the darkness of prison, she sees, there are "bold and happy" men and women who "seek the true path" and even know that they are on it and their "time is coming."[15]

A "Mirror of Truth" in the Name of "Man"

Looking back in history, and across cultures, we see almost universal talk about the inherent dignity, even sanctity, of the human being. There have been no end of arguments about the qualities of the human personality that endow people with dignity and thus rights (is it the human capacity to reason, our moral sense, free will?); its reach (is it inherent in all people equally no matter their station or effort?); its origins and development (is this a historical idea born in the ancient world, created by Renaissance humanism, asserted first during the Enlightenment, or not limited to the West?); and its social, legal, and political implications (what sort of society can fully recognize, defend, and advance the dignity of the human person?).[16] In Russia, although the idea reaches back to scriptural recognition that God created Man in His own "image" and "likeness," with all the ethical demands that derived from this, the richest development of ideas about human dignity arose in the eighteenth century, echoing the spirit of the Enlightenment. Among its most influential proponents was Nikolai Novikov. He was Russia's leading journalist, editor, publisher, and printer during the reign of Catherine the Great (who, though herself an advocate for Enlightenment ideas, lost patience with Novikov's criticisms). Precisely because he was less an original thinker than a popularizer of ideas beginning to circulate, he deserves our attention.

His first efforts were satirical: criticizing failures to realize the good, as defined by both rationality and morality. He mocked landowners, for example, who did nothing useful for society and treated their serfs as less than human. His criticisms were not revolutionary: his ideal was a "patriarchal utopia" of morally enlightened and caring masters and rulers in a society united for the common good.[17] But at the heart of this modest challenge to the status quo was a subversive moral vision of equal human worth.

Novikov was unsure how far to press his criticisms, unsure whether the lightness of satire was adequate to the seriousness of the problem, unsure about the competing claims of secular humanism and religion in justifying criticism of the existing social order. The terrifying peasant uprising of 1773–4, known as the Pugachev rebellion, may have pushed Novikov toward more radical conclusions about what was needed to overcome human evil and build a society of harmony and love. Freemasonry helped move him toward a more utopian vision of possibility. In Freemasonry, Novikov found a cosmopolitan world of enlightened men who shared his discontent with the limited and degraded reality of the world as it was. Among Freemasons, he found a community committed to spiritual and moral self-perfection, which included a moral duty to serve one's fellow human beings as God's creatures. The Masonic lodge was itself a type of "utopian space" in the present: nurturing alternative spiritual, social, and moral ideas; bringing "the future into the present" in its closed and secretive world. The Masonic goal was a "new world," a "Kingdom of God" where the fallen and debased person of the present would be replaced by the "true Man," by a "new Adam." Obviously, their focus was on men.[18]

Novikov established a journal, *Morning Light*, that was like no publication seen before in Russia: a self-proclaimed "mirror of truth" filled with "moral writing" to "elevate virtue, so debased in this world, to its majestic throne, and to show to the world that vice, in all its nakedness, is vile and contrary to human nature." At the heart of this crusade was the simple but powerful idea that "The human being [*chelovek*] is something lofty and worthy," that "heaven and earth, water, air, and fire, in a word, all of creation" has no meaning apart from the life of the human being.[19]

In a society where most people lived in conditions of serfdom that were very near to chattel slavery, in a polity where autocratic rulers had no accountability before citizens because they felt themselves to be closer to God than Man, in a culture where most people were unable to gain even elementary education, these were dangerous words, a vehement challenge to the world as it was in the name of the world as it should be—the core of the utopian method. Catherine the Great may have perceived the danger: she had Novikov arrested and imprisoned, his publishing house closed, and his publications destroyed. Catherine's son, Paul I (who hated his mother), set Novikov free, though he remained a broken man until his death in 1818.

"The Fate of the Person Is More Important Than the Fate of the Whole World"

The 1830s and 1840s were remarkable decades in Russia of intellectual ferment around the person, social morality, and the future. The monarchy of Nicholas I was more than usually rigid and authoritarian, evincing a dangerous combination of moral disdain for sinful mankind, fear of social vitality and change, and belief in the necessity and righteousness of disciplining order by the strong hands of state, church, landlord, and master. In contrast, the emerging Russian "intelligentsia" had faith in human capacities and worth, the benefits of civilizational progress, the transformative power of ideas, and the moral necessity of freedom. Although the meaning of the term "intelligentsia" has been much debated by historians, a brief but generally accepted definition looks roughly like this: intellectually engaged individuals (no matter their level of education or their profession) who, in the name of lofty and perhaps universal principles, stood against what they judged to be any political and social order that violated those values.

Although the term was coined only in the 1860s, the intelligentsia emerged powerfully in the 1830s and 1840s, if not before. There were few of them: looking back, Alexander Herzen felt that "the Russia of the future existed exclusively among a few boys . . ., so insignificant and unnoticed that there was room for them between the soles of the great boots of the autocracy and the ground." But their influence would be enormous, not least because they embodied "the learning of all humanity."[20] Among forerunners, one might consider not only Novikov but also Alexander Radishchev (famous for his brilliant narrative on the inhumanity of serfdom, *Journey from St. Petersburg to Moscow*, published in 1790); the "Decembrists," who in 1825, having been meeting in secret societies, attempted to prevent Nicholas I from coming to power in the name of a more humane and liberal society; and Pyotr Chaadaev, whose "Philosophical Letters" (published in 1836 though written years earlier) were "a merciless cry of pain and reproach" against the debased condition of the Russian nation and spirit, which "shook all thinking Russia," Herzen recalled.[21] These and other early *intelligenty* were silenced by the monarchy: Radishchev was arrested and exiled to Siberia; the Decembrists were exiled and their leaders hanged; Chaadaev was declared "mad" and placed under supervision.

Chaadaev's pain and despair about Russia's past, present, and future stirred hopeful answers. One path of hope looked to Russia's past for a guide to the future. The "Slavophiles" looked to a time before Westernization—and to isolated rural communities where the West had not yet done much damage—brought to the Slavic worlds destructive individualism, calculating rationalism, and an increasingly coercive and alien state. They have been called "retrospective utopians," though it was not really the past that most interested them, and "conservative utopians," though they were not conservatives in the sense of opposing change. They sought a future very different from the condition and direction of the present: a society in which the human personality could thrive in freedom, with a rich inner life, united in communion with others.[22] Another path, attractive to many more educated Russians, was associated with Alexander Herzen, Mikhail Bakunin, Vissarion Belinsky, and other "Westernizers," who believed Russia's future depended on uniting with European civilization, though they could be as critical of the social failings of the

West as they were of Russia's failure to embrace the humanistic values of European civilization, especially the values of individual human dignity and rights.

The orientation of the Russian intelligentsia was strongly moral, inspired by a belief in the sanctity of the human being, loathing for every condition that limited and crushed the human personality (*lichnost'*), and visions of a redeemed new person in a new society. Slavophiles imagined a new person rooted in a restored native culture and in revitalized communities, a harmonious and holistic human personality that would replace the egoistic and calculating individualistic self of Westernized societies of the present. Westernizers embraced the human personality as the existential and moral basis of their critique of given reality and as the foundation of a road toward a world of freedom where the human spirit could reach its greatest potential. Both sought a more human world that yet existed "no place." For some, the ideal was destiny—the working out in history of reason, nature, or God. For some, the ideal was an expression of human freedom to understand and create the good in a world of uncertainty, contingency, and chance.[23]

Belinsky exemplified these beliefs and hopes. An essayist, literary critic, and editor for important magazines in his day and one of the leading "Westernizer" intellectuals, he was unusual among Russian intellectuals of the 1830s and 1840s in not coming from the landed aristocracy. His father was a small-town doctor and the family lived often on the edge of poverty. He attended university, rare for men of his class, with government support. In 1847, Belinsky wrote a remarkable letter to the writer Nikolai Gogol. He was provoked by Gogol's repudiation of the social criticism in his own earlier writings, which Belinsky had much praised as a critic. Now Gogol proclaimed the ills of the world as due to individual moral weakness rather than social conditions and looked to religion as the only salvation. Belinsky chastised Gogol for having "injured" his readers' "feelings for truth, for human dignity." In Belinsky's words:

Russia sees its salvation not in mysticism, asceticism, or pietism, but in the achievements of civilization, enlightenment, and humaneness. Russia needs not sermons (she has heard enough of them!) nor prayers (she has repeated enough of them!) but the awakening in the people of a sense of their human dignity, lost in the mud and filth for so many centuries. She needs rights and laws in accord not with the teachings of the Church but healthy thought and justice .... Instead, she offers the dreadful spectacle of a country where people traffic in human beings without even the crafty justification used by American plantation owners who claim that a negro is not a human being [*chelovek*].[24]

Belinsky said of himself that "for me, to think and to feel, to understand and to suffer, are one and the same thing."[25] What brought together these ways of perceiving was the ultimate moral question: the true and transcendent worth of the human person and the "mud and filth" in which actual men and women lived.

Belinsky explained this new understanding, which was the recent outcome of an intense intellectual struggle within himself, in letters to his friend Vasily Botkin in 1841.[26]

The time has come to free the human person [*lichnost' chelovecheskaia*], which already suffers enough misfortune without this, from the vile fetters of a reality not justified by reason.

The fate of the subject, the individual, the person [*lichnost'*] is more important than the fate of the whole world.

The Universal without the particular and individual exist only in pure thought. In living and visible reality, it is only a dead masturbatory dream .... What is it to me that the Universal exists when the individual person [*lichnost'*] is suffering?

On this moral foundation, Belinsky launched an unrelenting assault against everything in social reality that violated the dignity of the person: poverty, prostitution, drunkenness, the arrogance and self-complacency of power, bureaucratic indifference, cruelty toward the less powerful, domestic "tyranny," and violence against women.

Against the darkness of present reality, he declared, "my god is negation!" And negation will open the doors of possibility:

> There will come a time . . . when there will be no husbands and wives but only lovers . . . . Woman will not be the slave of society and of men but, like men, will be free to follow her inclinations without losing her good name . . . . There will be no rich, no poor, neither kings nor subjects, but only brothers, only people.[27]

This was the utopian rage and utopian hope—and more than a hope, for it stood on a faith that reality itself was moving toward this new life—that animated Belinsky's letter to Gogol and that led him to socialism: a social rather than individualist path toward the freedom and fulfillment of every person.

"New Women": Dignity and Freedom in Life and Love

The desire for a new world where a woman might "follow her inclinations" without fear of censure was evident already by start of the nineteenth century in the intellectual and emotional lives of some Russian women.[28] From the 1830s, an important influence was the life and work of George Sand, who boldly challenged the world as it was, which restricted women's self-realization as human beings. Not least, Sand demanded "freedom of the heart," not limited by social conventions nor debased by sensuality without love. Belinsky and Herzen were among the influential men who echoed Sand in their writings. But her greatest influence was on women, who daily experienced the social, personal, and moral limits of being female in a man's world.[29] A growing number of elite young women began to turn away from normative expectations about gender, to refuse, as a woman in Herzen's circle wrote in her diary, "to concede anything to society, not a single desire, not a single conviction, not a single impulse to love."[30]

In the 1860s and 1870s, theory and private experimentation evolved into public practice. Russian women seeking fulfilling public lives were studying at European universities (especially medicine) or at new "Higher Courses for Women" in Russia, working as doctors, and, most famously, joining underground revolutionary organizations where many took active roles. "These women brought moral fervor to everything they did," Barbara Alpern Engel argued in her study of women of the intelligentsia in nineteenth-century Russia. At the intellectual heart of that moral fervor was the equal worth of every person. In the name of this principle, women were determined to live radically new lives, freed of the traditional bonds of parents, husbands, and children.[31]

The *nigilistka*, the female nihilist, was the most visible and mythologized image of the Russian "new woman" in those years. Few "nihilists," men or women, accepted the label. Not because they did not reject all established authority that was not justified by rational argument but because they rejected the world as it was in the name of positive values, especially the dignity and natural rights of the human being. In the words of Sergei Kravchinsky, who participated in this movement, "nihilism was a passionate and healthy reaction . . . against the moral oppression of the human personality [*lichnost'*] in its private and inner life."[32] And they were determined to go beyond words. As Chernyshevsky said of them, they were committed to bring as much as they could "from the future into the present," in their own lives. For women, patriarchy added another thick layer of "moral oppression" to that experienced by men, especially in matters of gender, love, and sexuality. In the utopian mode, they refused to accept what was given as the only reality possible.

"New women" brought the future into the present in everyday ways. They rejected the norms of women's fashion—the flouncy dresses, elaborate hairstyles, jewelry, and cosmetics meant to highlight middle-class and upper-class women's kept leisure and decorative femininity. They favored short hair and simple dark dresses. They walked in the streets unescorted. Many young women quit their parents' homes and shunned marriage, notwithstanding the great difficulty of a woman trying to survive on their own without a supporting (and usually subordinating) man. Sexual freedom, for many of these women, meant not so much "free love" as freedom *from* sex and love. Their deliberately coarse manners and plain clothes were a purposeful negation of a femininity that marked them as sexual objects. They wanted to be treated as human beings, rather than defined and limited by their gender. But social reality pushed hard against their desires. Without the protections of family, they faced poverty, sexual assault, and the painful censure of a society increasingly intolerant of nonconformity. As a result, many liberated Russian women in those years accepted conventional personal lives as wives and mothers but sought to sever the Gordian knot of the present by joining revolutionary organizations and even engaging in acts of anti-state terrorism, hoping to disrupt the whole system.[33]

Vera Zasulich was one such new women. We enter her story at its dramatic zenith. In January 1878, Zasulich walked into the office of the St. Petersburg city police chief and governor, General Fyodor Trepov, who was receiving petitioners, and shot him point blank, severely wounding him. Immediately, the guards began to punch and beat her, to such an extent that they thought they might have killed her. Her trial was a national sensation. Her acquittal by a jury, which found her action morally justified, was even more sensational. But this was a story also with familiar themes: human dignity, morality, and the clash between reality as it was and reality as it should and therefore must be.

As a girl, sent by her mother to live with rich relatives after the death of her father, Vera discovered the Gospels. She found Christ "good and kind," she recalled in her memoirs, and much better than the harsh Father who abandoned Him to human sufferings. She soon lost her formal "faith" (*vera*), though Christ remained "engraved in my heart." She replaced dreams of escaping harsh reality into a heavenly "eternal life" with dreams of a "life to come on earth." At school, she imagined her future revolutionary "exploits" and wearing a beautiful "crown of thorns" on a path of heroic suffering, struggle, and death. At the age of seventeen, she moved to the capital, St. Petersburg, found work sewing book bindings, and entered underground revolutionary circles. There she met Sergei Nechaev, whose "Revolutionary Catechism" demanded that revolutionaries tear themselves free from "every bond to the social order and the civilized world, from the laws, customs, accepted conventions, and morality of that world," in order to prepare an "impassioned, total, sweeping, and merciless destruction" of the old world and bring about the "complete liberation and happiness of the people."[34] Her efforts to help his revolutionary organizing led to her arrest, imprisonment, and exile in 1869 at the age of twenty.[35]

In the summer of 1877, back home in St. Petersburg, she read in the papers about the harsh beating and whipping of a political prisoner, Alexei Bogolubov, for failing to deferentially remove his cap when Trepov was passing through the prison yard. At her trial, Zasulich told the court that after reading this news and hearing more details from friends, including that Trepov ordered the punishment, "I decided, even if it cost me my life, to show that no one who abused a human being [*chelovecheskaia lichnost'*] that way could be sure of getting away with it." She recognized the moral dilemma: "It is a terrible thing to raise one's hand against another human being . . . . But I could find no other way to draw attention to what had happened." When pressed by the judge, she emphasized that her action was not "revenge," nor did it matter whether she killed or wounded Trepov. "I wanted to draw the attention of public opinion to what happened and to make it less easy for someone to commit such an outrage against human dignity." Her defense attorney elaborated, in his summation before the jury, that outrage at such brutality was felt by "everyone for whom feelings of honor and human dignity are not alien," and so Zasulich should be judged not according the letter of the law but "from another point of view . . . more human": that of reason, fairness, morality, the human personality (*lichnost'*), and human dignity. Zasulich acted, her attorney told the jury, from "a sense of deep, irreconcilable outrage for the moral dignity of mankind."[36] The jury agreed, and she was freed. The tsar thought otherwise and ordered her arrested again. Zasulich hid with friends and supporters and then fled to Switzerland, where she became an activist in the emerging Russian socialist movement.

Alexandra Kollontai was six years old when Zasulich shot Trepov. Like an increasing number of young women growing up in Russia in the 1880s and 1890s, she was determined to be a free and autonomous person, to live and love as she wished. Changing social mores made this possible. Like the fictional Vera Pavlovna, Kollontai freed herself from her parents' home and the traditions of her noble class by marrying a man whom her parents did not approve of. But then she left behind marriage as well, though not romantic and intimate love, for a life beyond the limits of domesticity.[37] Her first public act was to write a book on child-rearing (she was herself a young mother), arguing that parents' chief task is to nurture children's independent personality, preparing them to challenge society's accepted beliefs and search for a path toward social "perfection."[38] Active in workers' and socialist circles, she became known for her arguments about the oppressive restrictions on the individual personality, especially of women, and about the coming "new society," "new morality," and "new people."

Like most Marxists, Kollontai rejected the Kantian idea of universal moral absolutes and also the Nietzschean idea that the will of exceptional individuals, especially the future "superman" (*sverkhchelovek*), can create new moral norms—ideas popular among Russian intellectuals at the time. Rather, she believed, ethics derive from social relations and experience. As a result, present-day society is dominated by the "bourgeois morality" of egoistic individualism. The future, however, will be shaped by different social relations and a different class—socialism and the laboring majority—and so a different morality. Still, even in the capitalist present, workers' everyday experiences and interests are leading them toward a new morality based on "solidarity, unity, self-sacrifice, and the subordination of personal interests to the interests of the group." Yet this is not yet the truly free future. In that new world, a society without competing individuals or antagonistic classes or compulsion, there would be a "social atmosphere" in which will arise an entirely "new person," "a higher moral type of person, now inaccessible to us," "the harmonious, whole, strong, and beautiful image of the true superman."[39]

Kollontai differed from most Marxists in insisting that a critical view of the present and the path to a liberated future demanded attention to the emotional and intimate life of men and women. If revolutionaries did not pay more attention to love and sex, she argued, humanity will not reach that "alluring, flickering goal in the distance—all-sided liberation in a renewed world."[40] In the given world, the typical male, "overlooking the complex vibrations of love's sensations, follows only his pallid, monotone, physical inclinations." But almost every woman knows not to "seek in sexual intercourse completeness and harmony." The conditions and values of our present life, she argued, degraded the "love act" from "the ultimate accord of complex spiritual feelings and emotional experience" into something "shameful, low, and coarsely animalistic." Kollontai saw hope, however, precisely in the "tragic" modern condition: for the darkness of present reality, she argued dialectically, encouraged a "longing for the still unrealized future," for a "new morality" that will allow the "new woman," free in love and labor, to be a "self-valuing" and socially respected "woman-person" (*zhenshchina-lichnost'*).[41]

Socialism: For Individual and Community

The social reach of ideas about the dignity of the person, the liberation of women and men from oppressive norms, and the moral necessity of a society that nurtures these conditions continued to grow. By the early twentieth century, widely read newspapers and magazines viewed problems of modern everyday life, such as prostitution, domestic violence, hooliganism, drunkenness, and suicide, as resulting from low regard for "human dignity" and lack of "respect for the person" (*lichnost'*) in Russia. So much of present reality, it was said, "degraded," "insulted," and harmed the person.[42]

Working-class Russians echoed and intensified this refrain. In labor protests, workers demanded that they be treated as equal human beings. In the trade union press, which proliferated after the 1905 revolution, hundreds of articles, essays, and letters voiced moral outrage that workers were treated as "animals," "cattle," "machines," and "slaves." Workers demanded respect for their "human personality" (*lichnost' cheloveka*) and "human dignity" (*obshchechelovecheskoe dostoinstvo*).[43] There was immediacy and pathos in workers' writings, for the indignities were tangible in their everyday lives, doubly so for working-class women. Their voices, especially when they turned to poetry to express their thoughts and feelings, were filled with pain and moral injury: "the life of a worker is a chain of suffering / A river of sweat, a sea of tears." Increasingly, they voiced rage and a desire for revenge: "I am anger and vengeance . . . Where are lies and darkness? / I am their scourge / I am a sharp knife."[44]

Socialism was a logical conclusion to these arguments, as it had been for Herzen, Belinsky, Zasulich, and others. Russian socialists saw no contradiction between elevating the human individual and championing community and collectivism. On the contrary, the reciprocity of self and collective, each benefiting the other, was a central belief. As the Marxist philosopher, and later People's Commissar of Enlightenment, Anatoly Lunacharsky put it in 1904, the human self would be fully realized only when people outgrew the narrow, self-centered, individualism of bourgeois society and embraced a "broad-spirited," "macropsychic," individualism where the personal "'I'" is at one with a broad and enduring 'we.'" This was a practical but also "moral" interdependence: to ensure the "dignity of the human being" and the richest development of the "human personality" (*lichnost'*).[45]

There was a danger here, already evident in the early Soviet years but inescapable by the 1930s. As ideologists championed "the beauty of collective happiness" and the abolition of "petty-egoistic personal happiness,"[46] the "I" began to wilt in the face of the triumphant "We." Yevgeny Zamyatin's dystopian novel *We*, written in 1920–1 but long banned in the Soviet Union, satirized this disregard for the individual in Soviet society. Even the Bolshevik poet Vladimir Mayakovsky felt growing dismay at the radically collectivist ideology of the "proletarian culture" movement: "Proletcultists do not speak / About the 'I' / Or about the self. / 'I' for the Proletcultist / Is utterly indecent."[47]

In an essay in the Communist Party newspaper *Pravda* in 1932, the influential writer Maxim Gorky argued that the Soviet "New Person" drew on "common human values" to "repudiate bourgeois animal individualism" and show that "the high integrity of individuality is closely bound up with the collective." The ultimate goal, he insisted, is a "new world" free of "the old superstitions and prejudices of race, nation, class and religion," a "universal brotherhood," where "every single person" enjoys "conditions for the free growth of their talents and capacities."[48] Gorky still held on to something of the old intelligentsia ideal of the value of human *lichnost'* in a society where collectivism was increasingly the only acceptable ideal. But he himself would play no small role, especially after his return to the Soviet Union later that year to be enshrined as the great Soviet writer, in promoting the Stalinist spirit of "We" over "I."

During the 1917 revolutions, especially after the triumph of Bolshevism in October, Gorky had worried about precisely this danger. Gorky's newspaper columns during 1917 and 1918, which he called "Untimely Thoughts," judged the unfolding revolution against the familiar touchstone of the worth and rights of the individual human being. The autocracy was overthrown, he argued in the spring of 1917, because of its degrading "treatment of the human being [*chelovek*]."[49] Now there is the risk that freedom is being corrupted by the free: "The great happiness of freedom," he warned, must not be darkened by "crimes against the person [*lichnost'*] . . . . We must understand, it is time to understand, that the most terrible enemy of freedom and rights is within us: our stupidity, our cruelty, and all the chaos of dark, anarchistic feelings that has been developed in our souls by the monarchy's shameless oppression, its cynical cruelty."[50]

After October, Gorky did not hesitate to criticize the new state for "not having the slightest conception of the freedom of the individual [*lichnost'*] or the rights of the human being [*prava cheloveka*]."[51] "The human being," he declared bluntly in December 1917, "is valued just as cheaply as before."[52] Like many others before, he imagined a new type of individualism, a socialist individualism, where the richest possibilities for the development of self and personhood are precisely in conditions of social solidarity and community, where the individual and the collective enrich one another. This was a moral stance. Gorky's vocabulary in 1917 and 1918 was filled with lists of virtues—freedom, brotherhood, truth, honesty, kindness, humaneness, friendship, love, reason, and conscience—and sins—cruelty, violence, lies, hatred, vengeance, cowardice, greed, envy, egoism, ambition, pettiness, and vulgarity.

Back in the 1890s, when Gorky was making a name for himself as a "writer from the people," this moral defense of the human being was already a leitmotif in his work. "You bastards," one character in an early novel chastises a group of merchants, "what have you made? Not life, but prison. Not order, but the human being shackled in chains. Suffocating, narrow, nowhere for a living spirit to turn. You are killing the human being. You are murderers. Do you realize you are only still alive because of human patience?"[53]

Gorky's most lyrical paean to the human person was his 1903 prose-poem "Humanity" (*Chelovek*, or "Person"). Gorky described the poem as his "Credo." It is a dream-like allegory about "the magnificent image of Humanity . . . tragic, beautiful Humanity," but also of a war within the human heart. On the one side are an army of "winged" embodiments of danger, Humanity's own creations, especially Falsehood, but also "old truths poisoned with prejudice," tired and powerless Hope, inert Faith, Hatred, Weakness, Melancholy, and Despair. On the other side is Humanity's beloved friend and ally, Thought, also winged. If Falsehood wins, and Humanity "believes that there is no happiness on earth higher than a full stomach . . . and petty comfort," life will remain vulgar and tedious. But when Thought awakens Humanity's consciousness, vague "desires" for a richer life will mature from a spark into a "fire in the darkness of the universe." The human self and the entire world will be in harmony. The human person will become "proud and free," able to "boldly look Truth in the eye" and face the "gloomy chaos of life on this long-suffering earth, crusted over, like a skin disease, with unhappiness, sorrow, misery, and spite." And when the time comes, Humanity will "sweep all this evil filth into the grave of the past." Then, possibility will know no limits. "Forward! And Higher!" will be the slogan for this coming era of human history.[54]

Even death, the ultimate enemy of personhood, might be overcome. In Gorky's *Chelovek*, Humanity allied with Thought overcomes Death, who turns out to be a less-than-fearsome foe after people realize their natural human capacities. This is a path beyond what the present has yet allowed, a path toward the human being becoming a god. A few years later, in his novel *Confession*, a believing collective exerts its spiritual power and faith to bring a paralyzed and dying girl back to life. To be sure, these are a mass of pilgrims beside a monastery, praying to the Mother of God. What they do not understand, Gorky makes clear, is that they *themselves*, "the people," through their own combined "will," cause the girl to rise and walk. Once conscious, the awakened people "fly over the earth" and in their "common flight" each individual is both "insignificant and great."[55] Or, as he would write in his newspaper column in 1917, "when people understand and feel their collective strength, even the realization of utopia becomes possible for them."[56]

Gorky's thoughts about overcoming death were shared with many intellectuals, artists, and even some scientists in early twentieth-century Russia. Death was judged a harmful vestige of the old that must be eliminated if one is to create a truly new world in which humanity would be freed from "necessity." Death is the ultimate anti-utopia, the definitive no-place against which human societies have fought back for millennia, whether with religious utopias of life after death, of heaven, and of resurrection; or with secularized spiritual faith that we live on through the memories we leave behind; or with even more modern efforts to prolong life through science. In literary metaphor and literal belief, in religion and science, the "utopia of immortality" has had especially strong appeal in Russia and the Soviet Union. And why, some asked, should this new life be selfishly limited to those living in the present? The philosopher Nikolai Fyodorov, who died in 1903, influenced many Russians with his arguments that the most important task facing humanity, if the human being is to become "what he ought to be," is for the world to unite to create the scientific, technological, social, and political conditions that will ensure immortality for the living and resurrection of the dead. This was not a utopian fantasy, he insisted, but a practical and realizable project once humanity turned its mind and energy to this essential "common task." His many followers agreed.[57] A variation, on the Marxist Left, was collective immortality: individual deliverance from death through embodiment in the collective. The death of the individual would lose its sting, they argued, for the individual would live on in undying collective humanity. All of these paths out of the absolute darkness of death—from physical immortality through science to the metaphysical union of individuals in the believing collective approached the individual in the same way: to be elevated, close to godhood, by human society.[58]

"How a Communist Should Live"

The Soviet "New Person" was an unstable and disjointed idea from the first years of Communism.[59] Even in the Proletcult, there was the ideal of hard, rationalistic, machine-like, individuals, but also lyrical, free, winged men and women. There were advocates of individual self-realization as the purpose of social solidarity, but also literally "selfless" collectivists who merged their "I" into the great "We" and felt each person to be "not an isolated separate being, but an entire ocean, embracing all of the souls that surround him."[60] There were visions of extraordinary, overachieving, heroic supermen—"fire-winged" "god-men"—of exceptional powers and will, rising above the common person, but who existed only to serve the people and even sacrifice themselves for the cause. Hard-edged rationality and a pathos of elevated emotions were both harnessed to the cause. When the New Soviet Person "fused" his "soul with machines," as the worker-poet Vladimir Kirillov famously wrote in his poem "We" (published in a journal called *The Future*),[61] there was nothing modest about this metaphoric act: he became a superman with the will and power to rise into the heavens, overcome death, and remake the world.[62]

Closer to earth than these cosmic visions was the everyday practical work of human development. After dark years of brutality and suffering during the civil war of 1918–21, Soviet life was filled with talk not only of economic reconstruction but also of remaking men and women for the new society. Talk of "cultural revolution" during the 1920s and into the 1930s, though its meanings and forms evolved, was premised on the necessity of changing human mentalities, values, and emotions, even as they worked to change the social conditions that made people as they were. There was growing attention to the reform of "everyday life"—*byt*, a small but dense Russian word at the intersection of everyday behavior, morality, ethics, feelings, and the sociocultural condition and fate of the whole society. Public lectures and writings by Soviet leaders throughout the 1920s were increasingly devoted to explaining "how a communist should live," how a "proletarian" should live, and the "old and new morality."[63] In the 1930s, too, many Communists considered the cultivation and

45

development of a new "socialist personality," a communist *lichnost'*, the most essential task.[64]

In moralizing tones, Communist leaders instructed workers, party members, and especially the youth about the everyday norms expected of them. In 1922, for example, at the fifth congress of the Communist Youth League (the Komsomol), Nikolai Bukharin (the editor of *Pravda*), Lev Trotsky (who was perhaps the most influential Soviet leader besides Lenin, who at the time was terribly ill), and others spoke of "moral" questions as key to the education and cultivation of new people ready to build socialism. In a long speech about the "communist cultivation of youth," Bukharin talked of "chaos" and "anarchy" in the moral life of the present, including "evil predatory individualism" along with "decadent" "psychological" moods, which harmed both body and soul. If we want to replace the old with the new, he told his young audience, we must "cultivate emotions"—we must "feel" as well as "know" what is right. And what is wrong, he declared, is what too many are doing now: showing how they have rejected the hypocrisy of bourgeois morality by leaping into lives of "sexual licentiousness."[65]

In a series of articles in *Pravda*, Trotsky also demanded attention to such "problems of everyday life" as work, family life, religion, sex, and drinking.[66] Even the most trivial matters were linked to the fate of the revolution, the liberation of the human person, and the path to the future. "Profanity," for example, was judged to be "the legacy of slavery . . ., of abjection, of lack of respect for human dignity, one's own and that of other people." Swearing from below expresses despair and lack of hope. Swearing from above expresses abusive power and feelings of superiority. The revolution will overcome these degrading legacies for "the revolution is above all the awakening of the human person" (*chelovecheskaia lichnost'*).[67] Indeed, Trotsky added, the ultimate "goal of communism," the "music of the future," is to develop "the physical and spiritual nature of the human being (*chelovek*)."[68]

All of this lecturing from above, which many listened to attentively, was accompanied by a mass campaign to correct the pathologies of everyday life: drinking, fighting, swearing, smoking, wasting time, washing and dressing negligently, domestic violence, sexual misconduct, rape, prostitution, crime, and even low tastes in literature, cinema, and music. In the 1920s, problems ranging from highly publicized cases of rape by gangs of young men, to drunken parties among Communist youth with jazz and dancing, to unhealthy personal habits (particularly smoking and swearing) were condemned, and the transgressors targeted in very public ways, including through performative "show trials" in clubs, schools, and factories.[69] In urban youth communes, which took shape independently of state institutions, activists believed they were building socialism in the everyday space of a shared home, creating the "new person" and the "new life" with radical approaches to gender, morality, love, sex, family, and the ever-thorny question of reconciling personal desires with the collective good. Within their walls, young Soviet "communards" joined the fight against hooliganism, drunkenness, promiscuity, disrespect for women, poor hygiene, swearing, and "street ethics" in the name of the transformed new person.[70]

These sins of everyday life were viewed as "vestiges of the past," not inevitabilities in human life, much less consequences of the present. They needed to be "purged." Communist party "purges" (*chistki*), while often political, were also efforts to "cleanse" (*chistit'*) the Party and the Komsomol of drunks, hooligans, decadents, egoists, abusers of power, anti-Semites, and the like. Few doubted that such everyday moral failings would vanish as the new life emerged. This was a practical utopianism, the creation of the new human being in modest steps, trying to practice in the present as much of the future as possible. But these first steps were thought to lead toward a flying leap in the open air of history, a revolutionary leap, as it was so often said, from "the kingdom of necessity to the kingdom of freedom."[71]

Everyone agreed that it was impossible to adequately imagine the future when living within the boundaries of the present. But some were willing to "speculate," if only to fend off frustration and despair. Trotsky tried to imagine the fully new person of the communist future:

The human being [*chelovek*] will become incomparably stronger, smarter, and more subtle. His body will become more harmonized, his movements more rhythmic, his voice more

47

musical . . . . The average human type will rise to the heights of an Aristotle, a Goethe, or a Marx. And above this ridge new peaks will rise.[72]

To those who might call this "utopian," Trotsky might have answered with his argument twenty years earlier that one must be a "pessimist of the present" and an "optimist of the future." Yes, present realities try to crush your dreams and visions. Present reality screams "Death to Utopia! Death to faith! Death to love! Death to hope!" But the optimist of the future defiantly replies, "you are only the present."[73] This critical orientation toward time and possibility, which we can trace across a century and a half of efforts to imagine the new person in Russia, is the method of utopia.

CHAPTER 3
THE NEW CITY

Cities, like dreams, are made of desires and fears.

—Italo Calvino, *Invisible Cities*

In 1919, Vladimir Tatlin was commissioned by the arts division of the People's Commissariat of Enlightenment to create a "Monument to the Third International." He designed a giant glass and iron tower to stand astride the Neva River in Petrograd. It was to be a usable building, with meeting rooms and offices, and a towering symbol of global communist aspiration. The project was developed in sync with Lenin's campaign for "monumental propaganda," which had been inspired by an unusual source for a Marxist: the early seventeenth-century utopian tract *City of the Sun*, written in a Naples prison by the dissident friar Tommaso Campanella. Lenin admired how the entire urban landscape in Campanella's utopian city is used for mass education. He may also have admired the planned, ordered, even authoritarian qualities of Campanella's utopia. The walls of the City of the Sun are covered with painted illustrations of the whole of human knowledge of the world—from the cosmos to geography, from human life to plants and animals. Lenin's decree in April 1918 launching the campaign was fairly conventional: to "tear down from the squares and streets" tsarist monuments that lack "historic or artistic interest" and organize competitions for new urban monuments. In his first draft, these monuments were to "reflect the ideas and feelings of the bright Russia of the future." Lenin revised those last words away from their lyricism and futurism to a simpler phrase: "the ideas and feelings of revolutionary laboring Russia."[1] Tatlin was in charge of the campaign for Moscow, the new capital, as head of the city's branch of the Commissariat of Enlightenment. But Tatlin's vision for a monument to world communism was very much what Lenin crossed out: brilliant, full of thought and feeling, and looking into the future.

Tatlin's tower was to be a colossus: a soaring, spiral, internally mobile monument, both utilitarian and expressive.[2] It would stand taller than the Eiffel Tower, then the tallest built structure on earth, and its arching base would stretch across the city's Neva River. Its iron structure would contain giant halls encased in glass walls, double-paned and vacuum-sealed for temperature control. The interiors of the building's three main stories would rotate in harmony with the cosmos: a bottom cube revolving on its axis once a year, a middle pyramid making a full circle monthly, and a top cylinder making one revolution each day. The first-floor cube was to be an enormous meeting hall for international congresses and legislative assemblies, the second-floor pyramid would house the Communist International's administrative offices, and the third-floor cylinder would be an information and communications center. Above these three main levels is a hemispherical glass room, presumably for radio and broadcasting equipment since the International office was to use every form of modern communications, sound and visual, in every language of the world, to send out its message (on overcast days, projected onto the clouds) (see Figure 3).

The forms of Tatlin's monumental tower were deliberately modern, urban, and aspirational. Tatlin and his team rejected the figurative art of Greco-Italian classicism, because its focus on individual heroes would be at odds with "the modern understanding of history" and with what the revolution needs, we are told in an accompanying pamphlet by Nikolai Punin. In contrast, Lenin's "monumental propaganda" had a traditional approach to history: the campaign replaced monuments to old-regime heroes with monuments to new heroes. In August 1918 the government released the official list: all dead Europeans or Russians, and all men apart from the progressive actress and theater producer Vera Komissarzhevskaya and the terrorist Sofia Perovskaya. The list included "revolutionaries" (the largest group) but also writers, poets, philosophers, scientists, artists, composers, and actors. The eclectic list was composed to illustrate a deep and broad history leading to Russia's revolution: from Spartacus to Marx to Chernyshevsky to Plekhanov

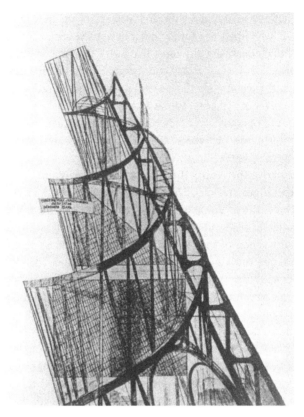

Figure 3 Vladimir Tatlin, Design for the Monument to the Third International, 1919–20. N. Punin, *Pamiatnik III internatsionala* (Petrograd, 1920). © SPUTNIK / Alamy Stock Photo.

("the father of Russian Marxism").[3] In addition, the utopian authors Thomas More and Tommaso Campanella were among names of revolutionary forerunners carved into an obelisk beside the Moscow Kremlin. Tatlin's monument turned away from this tradition of celebrating individual dead heroes. Nor was it a visual allegory with familiar symbols and images, like Konenkov's representation of a winged revolution. In Tatlin's monument, the medium is the message, its form the expression of a new vision and radical possibility.

The city was entwined with this message of the new. As Punin's pamphlet explained, the tower "must live by the social and political life of the city and the city must live in it." Like the "modern" city, the tower must be "necessary and dynamic." We see this modernist stance in the technology that moved its halls: the building is itself a gigantic machine (though in the architectural model, the revolving rooms were operated by a concealed boy turning a crank).[4] We see the tower's modernist vision also in its leaning spiral frame: "The entire form vibrates like a steel snake" united in a single direction: "to rise above the earth. The form wants to overcome matter and the force of gravity . . . . Straining its muscles, the form seeks an exit." This is the meaning of the upward spiral: "the spiral is the line of movement of the liberation of humanity." Not least, we see the modernist vision of the tower in its glass walls: "glass signifies the purity of the initiatives [of the International], their ideality, freed from the pull of materiality."[5]

Tatlin's tower has been compared to the Tower of Babel, the mythic symbol of a once united humanity that was determined "to build ourselves a city and a tower with its top in the heavens, that we may make a name for ourselves." God's thinking before he divides and scatters humanity across the earth is telling. He realizes that once again He needs to limit human hubris: "if this is what they have begun, nothing they have a mind to do will be beyond their reach" (Gen. 11:4-7). The Tower of the Third International would reunite humanity. The tower's cosmological elements, especially its movement with the rhythms of earth, moon, and sun, and its aspiration to free life from matter and earth, add to these utopian qualities. Glass architecture, as we saw also in Vera Pavlovna's fourth dream in Chernyshevsky's *What Is to Be Done?*, was a vision of unprecedented openness, freedom, natural light, and purity, the opposite of the Vera Pavlovna's symbolic dark cellar.[6] In other words, Tatlin's tower was utopian not mainly because it was impossible to construct, the narrow definition of utopia. It was "utopian" because it grasped toward possibilities that were "just out of reach."[7]

The Dream of the New: St. Petersburg

Utopian thinking has often imagined a renewed and transfigured city: from biblical visions of a "new Jerusalem coming down out of heaven" and "all things made new," the culminating image of the Christian narrative (Rev. 21:1-5); to medieval visions of a "blessed city of Jerusalem . . . constructed in the sky of living stones"; to the Russian patriarch Nikon's New Jerusalem monastery; to the "città felice" of Renaissance architects and philosophers; to Marxist futurology. Cities, Italo Calvino observed in *Invisible Cities*, are "like dreams . . . made of desires and fears." This allows "everything imaginable to be dreamed."[8] Still, this dream has never been free of worry and fear. It is not surprising then that the image of the city in literature has long been a "great reification of ambivalence": the city as perfection, the city as corruption; the city as rational order, the city as chaos and danger; the city as space of sociability and community, the city as space of alienation, exploitation, and violence; the city as vitality and possibility, the city as destroyer of lives; the city as Paradise, the city as Hell. The city is surely the greatest monument to human capacities—our best and our worst.[9]

The city is a material monument: idealism in stone, brick, metal, and glass. Architecture and city planning have often been characterized by a practical "will-to-utopia," as the American intellectual and journalist Lewis Mumford, later an eminent urban historian, described the architect's impulse in 1922: "The more that men react upon their environment and make it over after a human pattern, the more continuously do they live in utopia."[10] Historians of architecture have identified of "an optimistic architecture (of the ought),"[11] which has sought to overcome not only the harm caused by crowded, unsanitary, and disorderly cities but the contradictions of the city itself: to make cities places of both unlimited possibility and rational order, of individual freedom and collective life. Ernst Bloch called this a "wishful architecture" and wandered among the forms of urban wishfulness across world history: the pyramids, gothic cathedrals, American skyscrapers, garden cities, modernist "radiant cities," and more.[12] Architecture and utopia have long been allies.

St. Petersburg was precisely such a city from the time of its creation as a new capital for the newly named Russian Empire at the beginning of the eighteenth century. It was built on a marshy swamp at the edge of the sea precariously settled by scattered fishing villages. This empty space was ideally suited to Peter the Great's desire to create something radically new, unrestricted by the past or the present and dismissive of the limits of nature. The impossible terrain allowed him to join a long history of human efforts to "subdue" and "rule" the natural world, as the first book of Genesis proclaimed to be God's commandment and promise to humanity. Peter mobilized thousands of serfs, convicts, and prisoners of war to drain the marshes, drive oak piles into the ground, and construct a new city. Many lost their lives. Tragedy vied with heroism in the emerging story of the city, as it often has in the long human effort to rule nature and transcend limits.

St. Petersburg spoke in surveyors' lines and builders' stone of a radically different future for Russia. The turn away from the Muscovite past and native rural landscapes toward European modernity and cosmopolitan urbanity was not entirely out of the blue: Moscow already had a large neighborhood for foreign specialists brought to Russia during the reign of Peter the Great's father. Peter himself had spent much of his youth there learning new skills, including drinking and dancing. The designers of the new capital included the French architect Jean-Baptist Le Blond (made chief of the project for a new city), the Swiss-Italian architect Domenico Trezzini, and the Italian architect Carlo Rastrelli. Modern order was the primary design motif: rectilinear streets and avenues, geometric gardens and squares, and evenly proportioned neoclassic and baroque palaces and government buildings (tinted bright blue and yellow in the style of Europe's great metropoles) accommodating a human society of ranks and roles made visible in people's special uniforms. Nature, society, and people were all aligned and harmonized in strict order in this new city. Le Blond's general plan for the city, though not realized, was an elegant vision of geometric streets and gardens subordinating the irregularities of nature on this swampy edge of land, while also keeping external threats at bay with strong fortifications (see Figure 4).

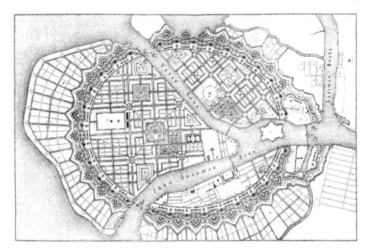

Figure 4 General plan for the city of St. Petersburg by Jean-Baptist Le Blond, 1717. © Art Collection 2 / Alamy Stock Photos.

Interpreting this new city became a cultural obsession in Russia, so much so that the actual city was overwhelmed by a "Petersburg text," the work of scores of writers, poets, journalists, and others.[13] A dominant theme has been contradiction and ambivalence—and as an interpretation not only of this particular city but also of the modern, the urban, and progress writ large. As a physical place, Petersburg was viewed as spacious, clean, and pleasing, defined by graceful modern European architecture, open spaces, linear streets, and granite-banked canals that channeled the unruly waters of marshes and rivers: signs in stone of civilizational order imposed on backward and unruly lands, nature, and people. But St. Petersburg was also viewed as a cold, damp, and dusty city, visibly defined and literally darkened by fog, rain, snow, floods, smoke, soot, and dirt. As a social and cultural space, Petersburg's landscape was viewed as graced by elegant architecture, gardens, and palaces, but also marked by cold stone facades and streets, stinking and rowdy taverns, hostile strangers and crowds, and every imaginable danger. The spirit and mood of the city and those who dwelled in it was free, joyous, energetic, renewed, and filled with dreams, but also tired, lonely, sick, feverish, tormented, depressed, melancholy, grieving, and sorrowful.

To pause at one classic example. When Fyodor Dostoevsky explored the streets of the capital as a journalist looking for impressions for his column, he observed that "one cannot take a step without seeing, hearing, and feeling the contemporary moment and the idea of the present." This meant modern life in all its contradictoriness: "dust and rubble" but also "becoming," youthful beauty blended with "fatigue, weakness, and dull melancholy," an atmosphere of "the new" that was also thick with "utter hopelessness."[14] In his great city novel, *Crime and Punishment*, his anti-hero Raskolnikov finds a peculiar pleasure in St. Petersburg's "stinking, dusty, city-infected air" and deliberately goes out into the streets "to feel even more nauseated," while the even more cynical Svidrigailov goes out into the "despondent and dirty" streets to commune with the city's strangeness, absurdity, and mad chaos.[15]

We are clearly in the twilight zone of utopia/dystopia—a place where opposites are interdependent and entwined, facets of the same perception, understanding, and vision. This is not the dystopia of utopia in power and therefore corrupted, its common definition. This is the "dystopia of the status quo," the dystopia of reality as it is, the lived experience that inspires and shapes every utopia. This is dystopia not as utopia's Other but its inspiration as well as its troubling potential.[16] We see this intersection of dystopia/utopia in much of the history of how cities have been experienced, especially in modern times. The dream that St. Petersburg was bringing light into darkness, civilization into backwardness, and order into chaos required a critical recognition of that darkness, backwardness, and chaos and a belief in the possibility of literally building a bright future.

Through "Gardens of Iron and Granite" and the "Hell of Smoke, Torment, and Death"

Urban newspapers and magazines in Russia in the early 1900s celebrated the civilizing and liberating effects of urban life. "The modern city," wrote one essayist about its psychological effects on ordinary workers, stimulated the mind and the spirit with the rich "complexities of city life" and daily proof of the benefits of the latest forms of social organization and technology. The salutary result was a modern mentality free of old prejudices and grounded in faith in "human capacity" (*sila cheloveka*, literally the strength of the person).[17] Some writers suggested that you could see this mentality even on people's faces.[18] Many writers associated the spirit of the city with the chance to experience the wonders of modernity: because of "the colossal progress of modern technology"—flying machines had conquered the air, submarines the depths of the sea, and x-rays the interior of the human body—urbanites became accustomed to "consider everything possible."[19] More cynical journalists mocked these modernist enthusiasms, though they recognized that the urban public were indeed infatuated with all things "new" and were sure they were on the fast road toward the "palace of the future."[20]

The press in those years was filled also with evidence to the contrary, with skepticism and doubt, even dystopian dread. Behind Petersburg's brightly painted European facades, journalists found a dark and labyrinthine world of back alleys and inner courtyards. Yes, they admitted, there is the story of human achievement in subduing nature, space, and time; but as soon as you "turn the page," you find greed, cruelty, violence, crime, and sin.[21] Yes, there is the "beauty of the modern" and the heroic whir of factories and machines; but if you look closely, you will see that the city is itself "a monstrous machine . . . ripping apart and devouring" people in its "insatiable maw." Yes, the vital life of the new modern city frees the individual and expands thought, culture, and industry; but these same conditions free the beast within every human being, showing the persistence of the ancient truth: "*homo homini lupus*" ("man is wolf to man").[22]

There were many reasons for hope and happiness in the big city by the turn of the twentieth century: the possibility of living "according to one's own will," freedom from restricting traditions (including in love, sexuality, and gender expectations), stores full of goods, opportunities for work and mobility, tolerance of unorthodox religious beliefs and practices, mass entertainment, the proliferation of civic organizations, access to information, legal and illegal movements for political and social change, and the simple pleasures of wandering the bustling streets. And yet, each one of these benefits could be interpreted, and frequently were, as signs of danger: egoistic and even predatory individualism, sexual debauchery and abuse, immorality untethered to universal values, crass consumerism, exploitation, and decadence.[23]

For many, it took an effort of will to keep in view the positive side of the new urban life. Social leaders encouraged citizens to push aside their "overcast thoughts," exercise positive "will," nurture a more "heroic personality," and feel more "audacious." Lenin, building a revolutionary movement, which required faith in possibility, constantly had to remind his comrades, even in the midst of the 1917 revolution, that "uncertainty," "pessimism," "hopelessness," and "despair" were intolerable and even "shameful" moods.[24]

The natural "heroes" of modern urban life, Marxists believed, were industrial workers. Through their own experiences, enriched by knowledge that the future would be theirs, they felt at home in the city like no other group. What the French poet Charles Baudelaire famously wrote about the archetypal bourgeois urbanite in the nineteenth century, the wandering *flâneur*, was thought to be even more true of the modern proletarian. For the *flâneur*, "his passion and his profession are to become one flesh with the crowd. For the perfect *flâneur* . . . it is an immense joy to set up house in the heart of the multitude, amid the ebb and flow of movement, in the midst of the fugitive and the infinite."[25] In turn, the "conscious proletarian," as the Marxists' hero, looks ahead to the "bright future" and so "clearly sees and understands that the modern city is an arena of struggle, the seething center where the liberating armies gather, struggling for the new world."[26] Workers learn to "love" factories and machines, for they realize that "in the whirl and noise of the turning wheels is born a new life, new thoughts, and a host of strong fighters for a bright life."[27]

But what of the experience of actual Russian workers? What was the relationship between utopia and dystopia in their views of the city before 1917? In history's archive, we have very few traces of the perceptions and judgments of the working-class masses. But we can still discover much in the voices of "conscious workers," though their perspectives were shaped by their connection to socialist movements. Feeling themselves to be both representatives and leaders, literate and awakened but having experienced lives of work and poverty, they communicated all they could of this to society, in newspapers and magazines. Very often, they turned to poetry, finding it more expressive than prose and more accessible for untrained writers like themselves to master. In what follows, I try to capture their responses to city life in an unconventional way: through two poems made by piecing together real lines, phrases, and words into a whole that never existed.[28] These are possible, but imagined, poems: utopian poems, one might say.

The first is an ideal type of the heroic, modernist, urbanist proletarian poem. The title of the poem is simply "The City," as many such poems were called:

From impoverished villages,
And decrepit peasant huts,
From hopelessness and sorrow
There is only one path:
Forward to the mighty city-giant,
To the realm of factories and machines,
Symbols of hope.

I walk in gardens of iron and granite,
Along parkways of stone,
Where I fell in love
With the flash of bright colors,
The clamor of street pleasures,
The festive roar of iron and steel.
I fell in love
With your stormy sea of shafts and wheels.

There, amidst the rattle of trams,
The glow of streetlamps,
And the thunder of machinery,
Is beauty and truth.

Russian Utopia

With awe,
In the radiant new city,
I grasp joy, pleasure,
Love, and the new life.
Merging with fire and metal
we struggle as one,
and sing of new days to come.[29]

From the same years, and the same publications, and in many cases
the words of the same authors, here is a different possible poem, also
titled "The City."

The city is merciless,
An abyss devouring its sacrifices.
The city poisons youthful dreams,
And fits you with deathly chains.
We live in dark cellars
As if in prison.
We wander

Through gloom and fog,
Stone corridors,
Harsh streets,
Sinister shadows,
And the sullen and soulless crowd.
The boulevard, with serpent's head,
Calls you to terrible sin.
A young woman
Leaps into the rusty canal.

In the city, I became alien to my own self,
And was nailed to the cross.
In the factories,
The voices of demons
Bellow with hellish thunder
Amidst fire, gas, and smoke.

How can I live in this Sodom,
This whirlpool of ambition and debauchery?
How can I live in this hell
Of smoke, noise, torment, and death?[30]

The "authors" of these poems were socialists, usually Marxists, and often Bolsheviks. Most wrote poems in both moods, for even revolutionaries often felt uncertainty and ambivalence. The darkness of the present may produce a utopian counterpoint of hope, even shape its repertoire of possibility; but hope and possibility come with no guarantees. Many socialist poets tried to resolve these contradictory feelings by thinking of these contrary images as "dialectical": opposed elements that drive the forward movement of history. The imprisoning hell of the urban abyss, in this way, becomes the womb where "hope," "love," and "the new life" can emerge. The same understanding led Lev Trotsky to insist that one needs both "pessimism of the present" and "optimism of the future,"[31] and the Italian Marxist Antonio Gramsci to speak of the need for "pessimism of the intellect and optimism of the will."[32] And yet, intelligence and experience in the present continually brought one back to the "hell" of reality. Marx and Engels wrote of revolution as a necessary "leap" out of the kingdom of necessity into the kingdom of freedom. In the meantime, it was easy to lose heart, no matter how loud one tried to "sing of new days to come."

After the October 1917 Revolution, Soviet cultural leaders worried about the dangers of workers dwelling on the darkness of urban life. Everyday life had not yet changed, of course—and the civil war brought to Russian cities new disorder, hunger, and want—but the hands controlling history had changed, so doubts should end. Sometimes these leaders directly warned workers to "purge ambivalence" from their writings, while recognizing its persistence. Most often, they simply proclaimed that ambivalence had vanished, for revolution alone had made the city new: "If previously the city was portrayed as an octopus . . . now the city seems quite different. The worker loves it." Now they "glorify the iron and concrete city," embrace its modern rhythms, and sing of their newfound "love for things and products and factories."[33]

This insistence on workers' happy confidence was not entirely a fantasy. In hundreds of poems by workers after 1917, we hear a great outpouring of adoration for the enchanting modern beauty of the big city: street corners, squares, sidewalks, posters, rooftops, electric lights, noise, factories, granite, and steel. Very often, though, these everyday charms paled in their imagination before hyperbolic images of the city as embodying the emergent and transcendent new: "a fire-faced Colossus," a "great iron-stone giant," a striding and talking creature made "entirely of steel and fire . . . breathing out cascades of light."[34] Dialectical images of the harsh city of the present giving birth to the city of the future, to a different and purified city, proliferated. And images of the Communist New City of the Future reflected a history of urban utopian thinking, including Chernyshevsky's crystal and aluminum city of dreams. As one worker-writer put it in 1924, the future city will be "gracefully elegant and crystalline in cleanliness."[35]

The Soviet cultural drive to purge ambivalence from the experience of urban life—a desire born of fear as much as hope—would silence many voices, but it could not erase the complexity of real experience. And until the late 1920s, it could still be expressed out loud. The trouble with imagining no ambivalence, the worker Nikolai Liashko argued, was that "too much lies in the heart of the worker writer," too much experience with the darkness and contradictions of the world as it is.[36] This was a refusal to be seduced by official utopianism. But it was also a utopian determination to look truthfully at the ugliness of the present. To pretend it did not exist was the utopianism of fools.

One could not ignore the persistence of vulgar commercialism, vain fashion, decadent leisure, sexual license, moral filth, and exploitation—"the spiritual poisons of the city," Liashko called them in 1918.[37] Few writers could ignore the worsening of poverty and hunger in Russia's devastated cities, but also the persistence of the old horrors of the city: violence and brutality, the debasement of women (including prostitution, now even more widespread as a means for survival), drunkenness and hooliganism among men, the coldness of the urban crowd, and "deep, secret torments."[38] At best, Liashko suggested, "modernity" (he used the Russian word "*sovremennost*", which can also mean "our times") is both heaven and hell, a roaring furnace fed with "passions and blood," a life of such radical "displacement and change" that "wonders grow into horrors and horrors into wonders . . .. Unexpected pains and joys . . . appear at every step."[39] Compromise with private enterprise and official tolerance for social and cultural diversity, including the darker sides of urban life, were part of the New Economy Policy (NEP) of the 1920s, which helped Soviet power survive. But NEP also sustained the old "poisons." We must remember that these were the doubts of communists, not anti-communist enemies of the revolution, the anxieties of proletarians not the "bourgeoisie." These were the voices of men and women who, in the utopian tradition, described the darkness of the lived moment not merely to interpret reality but to change it. They wished for "horrors" to grow into "wonders." But anxieties remained: that nothing will change, or that wonders might decay again into horrors.

The Transcendent City of Socialism

Marxists believed that socialism would obliterate the poisonous city of old and transcend the still suffering cities of the present. Perhaps no other political ideology or system has been so committed to the idea that one's physical environment can transform social experience and mentality. But even on the road to the future socialist city, urban planners and architects worked to bring as much as they could from the future into the present (to recall Chernyshevsky's call) by transforming urban landscapes. The "socialist city of the future" was talked and written about constantly in the 1920s and early 1930s.[40] The highpoint of radical design for the new city came during the First Five-Year Plan (1928–32), a time of forced industrial development meant to cut the Gordian knot of persistent economic backwardness though disruptive and sometimes violent social change, and a "cultural revolution" to shatter traditional social values and hierarchies. This has been called Stalin's "revolution from above," but it was also a chaotic revolutionary upheaval from every direction.[41] The American scholar S. Frederick Starr described these years as a "wild orgy of negation and innovation," not least in architecture and urban planning. This was a time with a strong will-to-utopia. "The architect," Starr noted, "could leap into the future even more easily than the novelist. Sitting at his drafting table, he could simply obliterate present reality with a few strokes of the pen and create a new world with a few more strokes."[42]

Among Soviet officials, Nikolai Milyutin was one of the most influential in urban development and planning, especially in his role as head of the Commissariat of Finance, which sponsored a number of architectural projects (Milyutin himself had once hoped to be an architect). In his 1930 book, *The Socialist City*, he compared the present city to the new city to come. In the capitalist present, the most advanced cities are congested "nightmares," "earthly hells" designed to serve the interests of concentrated capital and to maximize profits. The highest achievement of this model, literally, but also its proverbial "*derniere cri*," was the New York skyscraper. The future "socialist city" will be entirely different, a new type of city. Not least, the distinction between urban and rural will be erased. In this sense, the future city will not be a city at all, which throughout history has been defined as what the village is not: a gathering place, a magnet, a center of power, a stage for public action and drama.[43] Milyutin favored decentralized linear cities, with industrial, agricultural, and residential zones separated by park zones. Ideas about "green cities" and "linear cities," of course, were popular in the United States and Europe. But Milyutin declared these to be "the purest and most harmful utopia" as long as capitalism still ruled.[44] Such "disurbanism," as it was called in the 1920s, was widespread in Soviet thinking about the new city. Socialism would rid the world of backward and unhealthy villages but also of the congested earthly hells of the modern metropolis. Even Leonid Sabsovich, an "urbanist" (and an influential member of the State Planning Commission, or Gosplan), predicted in 1930 that the big cities that are now centers of political and economic life would soon be "the most backward, inconvenient, and uncomfortable places to live in the Soviet Union," overtaken in quality of life by a vast network of towns of 50,000–60,000 people connected to industrial areas and to one another by a national power grid and electric mass transit.[45]

Cities of the future, argued the influential Soviet sociologist Mikhail Okhitovich, would be "scattered" across networks in a "decentered" society where industry, agriculture, and human settlement are dispersed and enmeshed in nature. Life itself would be "destationized." Work, leisure, and rest will be less fixed by time and place than in the present. Society will be fluid, mobile, and open. A vast electric power grid and mass public transportation will allow industry, institutions, and people to free themselves from the crowded centers that capitalism produces. Dwellings, in such a world, will be mobile housing cells for one person—the family, of course, will have "withered away" under socialism—easy to assemble and disassemble for transport, that can attach themselves anywhere along the vast power grid.[46]

Only such a decentered and mobile world is emancipatory, insisted the editors of the Soviet journal *Contemporary Architecture*. Other approaches to the new socialist city are top-down "administrative utopias." Radical sounding "House-Communes," they boldly declared, were just "barracks" under a different name, not revolutionary rethinking of the city. Echoing arguments about the new human being whose individuality and personality (*lichnost'*) are enhanced by communal connections to one another, disurbanists designed living environments that transcended both "bourgeois, anarchistic individualism" and an oppressive collectivism that crushes individual will, desire, and freedom.[47] As Okhitovich put it, in terms quite typical at the time, "one cannot oppose the individual person (*lichnost'*) to the collective nor vice versa. The stronger the collective ties, the stronger the individual person . . . . The stronger the person, the stronger the collective."[48]

A "green city" proposal by Mikhail Barshch and Moisei Ginzburg envisioned Moscow transformed into a "grandiose park" with socialized services (from cafeterias and laundries to education and daycare), modern technology (mass transit, electricity, radio, telephone, television, automobiles, airplanes), and cultural facilities (including cinema and sports), but also open spaces, greenery, fresh air, and plenty of sunlight. People will live in rationally designed, sunny, and airy individual housing cells, gathered along radial axes with warm connective walkways, able to see and access nearby nature as well as social services and transportation. Their proposal was "radical," they knew, for it sought to "eliminate the evils of the big city"—including the domestic servitude of women, always strongly associated with the old urban life—and erase the difference between city and country. But it was also, they insisted, an entirely "realistic and economical means for resolving Moscow's problems." Like Okhitovich and others, they emphasized that the driving mission behind all this was to "create conditions for the most favorable development and flourishing of each individual person [*lichnost'*]." Capitalism suppresses individuality and the "human personality." Socialist collectivism must not do the same, they warned.[49]

One of the most radical visions of the new socialist city was the work of Georgy Krutikov, a Soviet architect who designed schools, metro stations, and residential buildings in the 1930s. His diploma project, in 1928, was called "City of the Future." It is an astonishing work: structures floating above the earth, powered by nuclear energy, with one-person apartments (no patriarchy or domestic servitude there) whose residents travelled between their airborne homes and earthbound industrial and cultural zones in individual flying capsules with elastic shells, self-cleaning walls, foldable furniture, and the possibility of travel both on land and under water.[50] Some critics ridiculed Krutikov's "flying city" as mischievous "day-dreaming" rather than the serious architectural work the developing economy needs[51] (see Figure 5).

One might respond by arguing that this critique misunderstands the utopian impulse and its critical functions. At the time, Lewis Mumford, the historian of cities and utopias, observed that "only a lunatic would refuse to recognize the physical environment." The complication is that our understanding of the physical world continues to change, sometimes radically. So, utopias that imagine what might look like "impossible castles in the air" can show us the folly of our limited views of reality.[52] Krutikov's teachers and judges responded to critics similarly: the point is not "to build the future city today" but to seriously address complex "scientific research problems," which must include "speculative formulations" that are "utopian" only for the immediate present. In other words, this is utopia as we have been defining it: a critical method to stimulate the contemplation of possibility.[53] Krutikov's future city was a project to suggest new forms

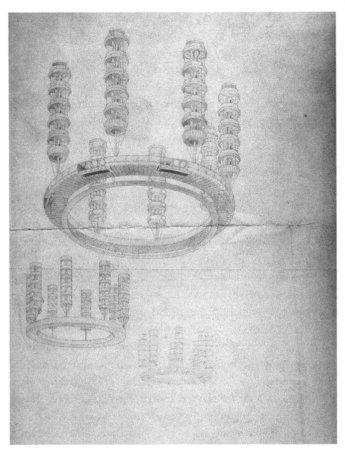

Figure 5 Communal residential blocks in the sky. G. Krutikov, "The City of the Future," 1928. Public Domain.

and new directions in material life, to raise questions, to open up possibilities, to challenge mentalities limited by existing experience. Krutikov studied the recent history of technology and especially transportation. Splitting the atom to release energy would be proven possible in a few years. And even now, Krutikov argued visually in his diploma project, the development of trains, automobiles, mobile homes and camping vehicles, airplanes, airships (dirigible balloons), ocean liners, and submarines—all building on a history of human "conquest of new spaces and new horizons" and "humanity's aspiration to rise above the earth"—made movement away from grounded and fixed abodes a logical and entirely realistic direction for architecture and city planning. What was once completely utopian, he argued, had become part of everyday reality. One should not be too hasty to dismiss such proposals as "utopian fantasy."[54]

The Communist New Rome

Standing enormous at the heart of the "new Moscow" was to be an awe-inspiring skyscraper showing the world what the socialist new city and new society really stand for. The idea for such a structure went back to the first meeting of the All-Union Congress of Soviets in 1922, held in the nineteenth-century Bolshoi Theater, when Sergei Kirov declared that the newly founded Union of Soviet Socialist Republics needed not only a more spacious and suitable place, a "palace," for delegates from across the Union to meet and work but an architectural monument that would express the meaning of the revolution and communism for the entire world.[55] Serious planning began only during the First Five-Year Plan. A suitably symbolic location was found: the site of Moscow's largest church, the Cathedral of Christ the Savior, which was dynamited in 1931 to make way for construction. Architects from all over the world were invited to submit designs to a competition. Among Russian entries, Konstantin Melnikov, who was perhaps Russia's leading avant-garde architect, blended constructivist modernism with expressive symbolic form: a giant split pyramid with half the pyramid upended so that the broad bottom rose into the sky—representing overturning the old social order where the few ruled the many, but also symbolic of death and immortality.[56] The winning entry, by Boris Iofan, expressed a very different style, that of an emerging Stalinist orientation toward monumental grandeur, hierarchical order, and the authority of tradition.

The plan for the New Moscow, approved by the Communist Party in 1931, was for a technologically modern, hygienic, and grand city of the future. The entire city was to be an aesthetic public experience, surrounding citizens with beauty and a feeling that socialism was tangible and present. Widened streets, parks, and green belts were all elements of the plan.[57] This was very much a *public* utopia— little attention was paid to improving living conditions for ordinary Muscovites. Grand and relatively luxurious apartment buildings were built, especially along newly widened roads, but only for the Soviet and Communist elite. The most famous of these was the "House of Government" along the Moscow River close to the Kremlin, which was also designed by Boris Iofan. The new metro, on which sustained work began in 1932 and the first line opened in 1935, built miniature underground palaces for the people, with chandeliers, marble walls and floors, mosaics, and sculptures. The utopian aesthetic was explicit: the station lighting was designed "to create the illusion for passengers that rather than being underground, they were in a sunlit palace in an unknown location." The exception was the metro station for the "Palace of Soviets," where the lighting was to be subdued so that the space would be experienced as a portal to the gigantic and shining palace beyond.[58]

The New Moscow reached into the past to create the future. While the engineering applied the latest techniques, the aesthetics turned away from modernism: away from the unadorned and functionalist lines of constructivism toward "decorativeness" and classical traditions, especially those of ancient Rome. Articles in the authoritative journal *Architecture of the USSR* proclaimed "the new Moscow as heir to the architectural greatness of ancient Rome," examined the Roman heritage in detail, and linked specific new buildings in Moscow to Roman structures. Boris Iofan, the lead architect of the Palace of Soviets, had studied and worked as an architect in Rome from 1914 until 1924. He disliked modernism and his Palace of Soviets drew on sketches he had made of ancient buildings. Echoing the imperial Roman Forum, the Palace was to be part of a "Socialist Forum." As in Rome, architecture was to confer grandeur on the state and on its citizens.[59]

The new model socialist city also resembled, in both aesthetics and political spirit, Peter the Great's new imperial capital in the early eighteenth century and Haussmann's renovation of Paris under Napoleon III's Second Empire in the mid-nineteenth. We can also see commonalities with architectural plans for Nazi Berlin and Fascist Rome, also drawing on classical Roman models, though more modernist in their preferences for stark simplicity. Above all, they shared with Stalinist architecture the intent to create the psychological and aesthetic impression of grandeur, order, stability, and permanence. What was utterly rejected in the USSR in the 1930s was the radically "decentered" and "destationized" visions of earlier Soviet architects and city planners. Moscow was to be a stable and solid center. Moscow was to be where the future was most visible in the present, where Stalin ruled as the "great architect of communism," as he would later be called.[60]

One way to think about the political aesthetics of this emerging Stalinist architecture is as a form of "the sublime." What defines the sublime—here I am drawing on a mixture of classic definitions and twentieth-century adaptations—are experiences that give a feeling of enormity beyond the familiar (untamed nature is the classic experience, but some have included examples from art and architecture and cases of political power and violence), that are so immeasurably "huge and grand" (from Edmund Burke's definition) that one is transported beyond the ordinary and the everyday. The sublime overwhelms our comprehension and even our imagination, stimulates a visceral "thrill" that is both terrifying and ecstatic, and reaches beyond conventional beauty toward something that leaves us breathless, that "moves" us toward new sensations.[61]

One can see the sublime in Tatlin's tower, for example, and Krutikov's flying city. But the Palace of Soviets most deliberately sought to embody the sublime, though one increasingly turned away from radical imagination and the pleasure of perceiving something immense and transcendent, toward the sublime power of political majesty. Design proposals were altered to have more impressive effect. Iofan was regularly instructed, on occasion by Stalin himself, to make changes. The most persistent demand was "ever higher, higher, and higher," to borrow the refrain of the popular Soviet song. Like the Tower of Babel and Tatlin's tower, the Palace of Soviets must reach the sky and pierce it. Anatoly Lunacharsky, the former commissar of education, is said to have described it as "not an imploring gaze toward heaven, but, rather, a storming of the heights from below."[62]

A drawing of the final, approved, design depicts this awe-inspiring skyscraper, taller than the recently completed Empire State Building (then the tallest building on earth), with a giant statue of Lenin (deliberately more than twice as tall as the Statue of Liberty) stretching his arm even further into the sky, with airplanes and a zeppelin flying above and below him. The marching crowds and the individuals walking up and down the stairs are mere specks. (See Figure 6.) Karl Schlögel has emphasized the "sublimity" of this "gargantuan symbol," on top of which Lenin seems "hidden from the eye of mere mortals by a blanket of cloud" as he points into the open sky and the inviting cosmos.[63] Inside the building, participants would be similarly overwhelmed by the vast open spaces and thousands of paintings,

Figure 6 Final design for the Palace of Soviets, by Boris Iofan, Vladimir Shchuko, and Vladimir Gel'freikh, 1934. Public Domain.

frescoes, sculptures, and mosaics. But if the traditional sublime reminds us of the awesome power of the human mind to grasp the ungraspable, the Soviet sublime elevates society and the march of history but minimizes the individual and even humanity.[64] A worker in Andrei Platonov's unpublished 1930 novel *The Foundation Pit*—a story that seems prophetic of the great foundation pit for the unbuilt Palace of Soviets, its only actual realization, which was turned into a swimming pool in the 1950s until a copy of the demolished church was rebuilt in the 1990s—insists that it is the cosmic not the intimate, the collective not the individual, that matters in building the future, and that sacrifice is the main thing people can offer the future.[65]

But was this "utopian"? Scholars have typically described Stalinism as a "negation of utopianism," for it purged utopia of its spontaneity and experimentation, not to mention faith in actual living human beings. Stalinism, one historian concluded, inflicted on the Soviet imagination a "fantasectomy," a kind of mass cultural lobotomy that made it impossible to dream of possibilities other than those chosen by the Leader.[66] Katerina Clark, writing about the transformation of Moscow under Stalin, judges this naïve and romantic. "In some senses the thirties were more utopian than the twenties," she boldly argues. If we look at the global history of utopian writing, she reminds us, while we do see utopias that are "freewheeling and hedonistic," the classic utopia is "bounded and restrictive," often located in hermetic places such as islands, and obsessed with borders, policing, conformity, and purification.[67] Truly, there is no lack of limiting and controlling qualities in utopian visions for the "new city" from St. Petersburg to the "New Moscow." We tend to wish utopia to be refreshingly imaginative and liberating. And so we admire Tatlin's unrealized architectural vision for urban transformation and revile Iofan's for its anti-human, oppressive, authoritarian spirit. But were not both examples of utopia as (recalling Bloch's phrases) "summoning what is not," "penetrating the darkness" and "building into the blue"? Surely, yes, but perhaps not. Can we rightly call architecture and city design "utopian" if it is not a critical method, a challenge to the present, an interruption of the here and now? Is it any longer utopian if it is satisfied with the present, even a revolutionary present? Utopian knowledge, I have been arguing throughout this book, always feels that "something's missing" in the present, never ceases to challenge the limits of possibility, never stops bringing the unreachable future into the present.

CHAPTER 4
THE NEW STATE

There is no horror, cruelty, sacrilege, or perjury, no imposture, no infamous transaction, no cynical robbery, no bold plunder or shabby betrayal that has not been or is not daily being perpetrated by the representatives of the states, under no other pretext than those elastic words, so convenient and yet so terrible: "for reasons of state."

—Mikhail Bakunin, 1867

Deep in the dark February days of 1903, the last Romanov emperor, Nicholas II, hosted two costume balls at the Winter Palace. If we are willing to take play seriously, and to speculate on meanings that may not have been entirely deliberate, we can see in these winter dances ideas about political power, history, and the nation. We can even call these balls "utopian," as suggesting a vision of the ideal and of the possible and seeking to bring it tangibly into the present. But this was a future inspired by an idealized past. Guests were ordered to dress as if they were courtiers from the reign of Alexei Mikhailovich (1645–76), the last Muscovite tsar before the reign of his son, Peter the Great, who embarked on a revolution of Westernization. Hundreds of tailors were set to work making the elaborate costumes. Officers wore seventeenth-century military uniforms. The palace guards were outfitted as the old musketeers (*streltsy*). Nicholas II dressed as tsar Alexei himself, and his wife, Alexandra, as Alexei's first wife, Maria Miloskavskaya, rather than as the mother of Peter the Great, underscoring further the symbolic erasure of Peter. The royal couple worked with the director of the Hermitage Museum to ensure accurate reproductions. The tsar's scepter and fur-rimmed crown were not costumes, however: they were the originals brought specially from the Moscow Kremlin. After

Figure 7 Emperor Nicholas II and Empress Alexandra dressed as Tsar Alexei Mikhailovich and his first wife Maria Miloskavskaya, 1903. © Public Domain.

leaving the ball around three in the morning, Nicholas II commented in his diary: "the room looked very pretty filled with ancient Russian people"[1] (see Figure 7).

Playful experiments with clothing were just the surface of Nicholas II's turn away from the present, from two centuries of European modernization in Russia. It may not have been a coincidence that Nicholas II's Muscovite masquerade occurred during the 200th anniversary of the founding of St. Petersburg. Nicholas hated Peter the Great's capital on aesthetic, emotional, moral, and political grounds. He regularly complained of the capital's un-Russian aesthetics, moral decadence, bureaucratism, and the political unreliability of its cosmopolitan population. So he did all he could to bring "Moscow" into "St. Petersburg." As if determined to place himself physically in a different time, he preferred to live outside the capital, at Tsarskoe Selo (Tsar's Village), where, for additional atmospheric effect, he had a new church built in the Muscovite style. Judging the secular capital to be aesthetically and spiritually alien to the Russian heart, in 1900 he began a new tradition of annual Easter pilgrimages to Moscow, a symbolic return to the historic and sacred center of Holy Russia, "the cradle of autocracy," where he felt he could better enter into "communion" with the nation and the common people. "With the true children of our beloved Church," he explained, and "in the prayerful unity with My people [*narod*], I draw new strength for serving Russia."[2] Here Nicholas used another one of those widely used Russian keywords that mean so much more than can be translated by any single word. Most simply, *narod* meant both "the people" (especially the common people) and the "nation," indeed the connection between the two. On the political left, to talk about the *narod* was to tell a story about the exploited masses and thus the suffering nation. On the right, talk about the *narod* was a story about "true Russians," the unreformed and unmodernized Russian folk, embodying the nation and the national spirit.

The turn away from existing reality was enacted on an even bigger stage in 1913, the tercentenary of the founding of the Romanov dynasty.[3] Russian political life was in a long, slow-burning crisis, especially since the 1905 Revolution and the incomplete and contested political reforms that followed. Liberals, increasingly numerous and well-organized, demanded a society based on the rule of law, active participation by citizens in affairs of state and society, and greater social protections—a deepening of Russia's history of Europeanizing reforms. Socialists, increasingly influential among intellectuals and workers, demanded all of this plus social equality and citizens' economic power. Three hundred years earlier, in 1613, Russia found a solution to an even more threatening crisis, known as the "Time of Troubles": a long period of dynastic uncertainty, internal rebellion, and foreign invasion and occupation, leaving economic devastation, population decline, and deep social distress and anger. But, according to the nationalist story of these events, the Russian people united with leaders of state and church to expel the invaders, elect a monarch (a special "Assembly of the Land" chose Mikhail, the first Romanov tsar), and thus save Russia.

Liberals looked back across these three centuries to 1613 as a moment of political innovation and possibility: the emergence of a "new political concept," a new state ideal, previously "unimaginable"— in place of a ruler who "embodied the state in his person" and the tsar's personal interest as the only interest of state arose the idea of a nation-state separate from the monarch and embodying the will of the people and the nation.[4] Nicholas II and conservative ideologists favored a different story: that only the absolute and anointed monarch can embody the will of the nation and God. In the words of the remarkable official biography of Nicholas II that appeared at the beginning of 1913, "thousands of invisible threads extend from the tsar's heart, which, in the words of the Scripture, is 'in the hand of God'; and these threads stretch to the huts of the poor and the palaces of the rich . . . . The spirit of Russia is incarnate in her tsar."[5] The notion of a state distinct from the person of the monarch, it was argued, is an artificial theory imported from the West and unsuited to the Russian spirit. Of course, this was a reaction to existing political realities: since 1906, Russia had an elected parliament and laws guaranteeing civil rights.

In May 1913, Nicholas and Alexandra toured the heartlands of old Muscovy where the events of 1613 had taken place. Peasants, townsmen, and merchants flocked to see the tsar, to wade toward his passing yacht, to fall to their knees in his presence with prayers and patriotic anthems. Reporters admired the tears of love that were shed in the presence of the tsar. Nicholas wept in return. A foreign diplomat expressed his wonder: "What power! What unity of national feeling! All our constitutions are nothing compared to what we are seeing."[6] This is exactly how Nicholas felt. And he and his allies drew radical political conclusions: given the unique bond between tsar and people, what need was there for parliaments, elections, ministers, or even bureaucrats?[7]

Moral idealism, even moral absolutism, was a leitmotif in these visions of the perfect state and society. Everyone, from the tsar to poorest peasant, should live with virtue, duty, orderliness, devotion to others, respect for authority, piety. Dissenters were "evil," Nicholas II believed. During the 1905 revolution, the first great challenge during his reign to the political and social status quo, he declared the struggle to be between "good people" ("true Russians") and "bad people" (especially revolutionaries and Jews), as a conflict between "virtue" and "sin."[8] After the revolution of 1917, even on the eve of his execution in the basement of the house where he was held prisoner, Nicholas believed the revolution to be the work of Jews and other people alien to the spirit of Russia. But soon "the good, virtuous, and kind *narod* . . . will come to their senses."[9]

This mystical and moral vision of politics grounded in love uniting a diverse nation was not a gentle one. It was neither egalitarian nor voluntary and in no way excluded punishment of people who failed to love the tsar as they should. Politics was to be an extension of the old patriarchal ideal of the wise father who used a strong hand for the betterment of his wife, his servants, and his children. Love between tsar and people, Nicholas believed, did not exclude, indeed required, merciless force against his enemies, but also against commoners who were misled. Moral faith in one's righteousness can justify great violence against those deemed outside virtue: a tendency we see among revolutionaries as well as radical conservatives. But even when bringing lethal force against protesters in the streets, Nicholas II insisted, "My most fervent wish is to see My people happy."[10] His revolutionary opponents believed the same about themselves.

Order and Love

This vision of the ideal Russian state—loving in purpose, while awesome in might; spiritually at one with the people and devoted to their happiness, but with no limits on coercive power—had a long history. The Russian state was founded, according to the semi-legendary tale recorded in the earliest chronicles, when scattered Slavic tribes "invited" Vikings (called "Varangian Russes") to "come to rule and reign over us" for "our land is great and rich, but there is no order in it."[11] Government was for the sake of the good, and the good was defined as law and order. We might call this political theory, which would last for generations, perhaps to the present, the "civilizing role of force exerted from above."[12] Of course, definitions of what it meant to be "civilized" were debated and changed. And forms of acceptable "force" were debated and changed. But the model persisted. National catastrophes and misfortunes were explained as the consequence of a lack of unity of people and state. The extraordinary power of the Russian state was justified as both necessity and virtue.

In the eighteenth century, the idealization of the bonds of love between an all-powerful tsar and a devoted people and the ideal of the civilizing role of force from above were modernized. Catherine the Great (1762–96) organized a national commission to rationalize and reform Russia's laws, telling the delegates that her chief goal was "to render the people [narod] of Russia, to the extent humanly possible, the happiest people on earth."[13] She framed the tradition of love between tsar and people with Enlightenment notions of the common good and humane feelings. When confronted with a massive peasant rebellion and dissent by educated elites, she deployed the full force of the state to maintain her authority, for she believed that only autocratic authority could ensure Russia's progress and happiness. She dismissed alternative visions—democratic ideas of intellectuals like Radishchev and Novikov (see Chapter 2) and especially the vision of peasant rebels who imagined a truly good tsar who would free the people from serfdom, military service, and taxes, and give all the land for free to those who worked it—as "unrealizable and fanciful dreams," and she did not hesitate to crush them.[14]

Catherine's grandson Alexander I (1801–25) came to the throne expressing familiar tropes of "love" for "the good" and desire to assure "the happiness of our people." After his death, he was mourned as "Our Angel." But this "angel" also loved discipline, order, and military aesthetics. His contributions to the architecture of the capital were a series of neo-classical buildings, echoes of the Roman empire, marked by uniformity and orderliness, including a large barracks in the center of the city: "a military paradise of straight lines, of men in order."[15]

The most striking effort to create a military paradise in everyday public life was the creation of "military colonies." Alexander I was inspired by his visit in 1810 to the estate of General Alexei Arakcheev, whom he later put in charge of the effort to move millions of soldiers and crown peasants into colonies on the model of Arakcheev's estate. What impressed Alexander was a well-regulated life that seemed perfectly to combine military discipline with devotion to the good of the people through economic planning and social improvements. Alexander's reaction was emotional and aesthetic as much as rational: "This is a truly charming place," he wrote to his sister, thanks to "the order that prevails everywhere, the neatness . . . the symmetry and elegance that one can see everywhere. The streets of the villages here have precisely that kind of neatness for which I have been clamoring for in the cities."[16] Colonists were to live in identical houses along neatly arrayed streets, and to benefit from a well-regulated economy, abolition of landlessness and vagrancy, good hygiene, and modern educational and cultural institutions, but also active surveillance, policing, and discipline. European visitors felt, clearly sensing the utopian spirit, that they were entering "a terrestrial paradise" located in a completely new time and space, separated by "more than a century of civilization" from ordinary Russian villages.[17]

Conservative Russian ideologists defended the principle of "autocracy"—defined as "sovereign, unlimited, monarchical power, independent of state institutions, assemblies, elections, representatives, or officials"[18]—as most suited to the Russian spirit. They did not ignore the abuses of power across the centuries. But they emphasized the ideal. In 1811, for example, the writer and historian Nikolai Karamzin sent a lengthy historical and political essay to Alexander I, who was contemplating a "constitution" for Russia that would ground the monarchy in the rule of law rather than the monarch's personal authority. Karamzin appreciated the tsar's "generous hatred for the abuses of autocracy." But the solution, he warned, was to make the potentials of autocracy real rather than reject the order as unsuccessful.

> Russia, taught by long disasters, vested before the holy alter the power of autocracy in your ancestor [a reference to 1613, always a touchstone in these arguments], asking him that he rule her supremely, indivisibly. This covenant is the foundation of your authority, you have no other. You may do everything, but you may not limit your authority by law!

And this "covenant" was not a matter of law or even tradition for its own sake but of "virtue" and the people's happiness, and the best protection again quarrelling and selfish elites.[19]

During the reign of Nicholas I (1825–55), these ideas achieved full canonical formulation. The minister of education, Count Sergei Uvarov, elaborated a trinity of principles for Russian political and social life: orthodoxy, autocracy, and nationality. These were not three separate ideas, Uvarov insisted, but a "unified spirit" that stood against the dangerous folly of European political culture, which ignored "past and future, living only for the present."[20] In the conservative utopian mode, Uvarov's theorization of the Russian state ideal was precisely a repudiation of the present (Western modernity) by embracing the past (national traditions) as the source of a perfected future. The principle of Orthodoxy rejected Enlightenment belief in human reason and capacity, viewing divine truth and power, embodied in the Russian Orthodox Church, as the only reliable source of ethics and of salutary authority. The principle of autocracy followed naturally: because human beings are intrinsically weak and sinful, an orderly and happy society is possible only under the strong hand of a divinely guided monarch. Again, Russia's historical experience was said to have proven this: that strong rulers were needed to guard the country against external enemies and against the selfish and abusive passions of people as they are. This was not only a negative ideal: autocracy ensured progress and happiness. As such, it was to be not despotism but a paternal power united in harmony and love with the people. Mikhail Pogodin, a historian and leading supporter of these ideas, compared the founding of the Russian state, which was based on "love" (the "invitation" to rule and bring order), to Western states, which were founded on conquest and thus "hate."[21] Nationality (*narodnost'*) linked these ideals to the special character of the Russian people, the *narod*. As it was often said, the Russian people understand the necessity and value of their own submission to the strong loving hand.

In his manifesto announcing the execution of leaders of the anti-autocratic Decembrist rebellion of 1825, the new emperor Nicholas I drew upon these ideas to explain their failure:

This design did not correspond to the character or ways of the Russians. Concocted by a handful of monsters, it infected their immediate companions, with their depraved hearts and audacious dreams. But their ten years of evil efforts did not and could not penetrate further. For the heart of Russia was and always will be inaccessible to this . . . . In a state where love for the Monarch and devotion to the Throne is founded on the natural traits of the people . . . all the efforts of evildoers will be futile and mad.[22]

If each nation has its own unique "genius," as nineteenth-century theorists believed, Russia's national genius was believed to be this special bond of love and devotion between the people and the tsar. This ideal was rooted in history—real or imagined depending on one's point of view—and embraced as the only source for a truly moral and healthy state. It would heal the present and ensure a bright future.[23]

Virtue and the Common Good

What of those "mad" and "evil" "monsters" with "depraved hearts and audacious dreams"? The Decembrists, as they would be called after their attempted revolution in December 1825, were an unintended consequence of a century of efforts by the Russian state to nurture among elites a sense of public service to the nation inspired by European values of reason and national love. Moods and movements across Europe during and after the wars against Napoleon were also a catalyst. During the reign of Alexander I, a time of considerable hope among educated Russian elites, some liberal-minded Russian aristocrats came together in secret societies to seek the moral regeneration of society, enlightened progress toward the good, and happiness for the nation. The Statutes of the Union of Welfare in St. Petersburg, for example, emphasized its goal to be nothing less than "the eradication of vice and the spreading of virtue." This was felt to be a matter of social "justice," which meant the good of each and every person: "the common good of the nation absolutely demands the good of the individual." This was a natural right and a political principle. States may take various forms, they argued, but "virtue" must be "the pillar of the state," and the virtuous state must be devoted to "the good of the ruled." This is the only path that would lead Russia toward "greatness and prosperity."[24]

The "dignity and rights of man" was the essential foundation for the new state. According to a draft constitution written by a leader of the Northern Society—which grew out of the Union of Welfare and was responsible for organizing the military insurrection in the capital— every individual in the new state was to be "equal before the law," abolishing both the privileges of nobility and the bondage of serfdom, because "all men are brothers, well-born by divine will, born for the good, and simply people, for all are weak and imperfect."[25] A future code of laws drafted by a leader of the Southern Society anticipated a much stronger state to bring radical social change: equality before the law, the end of social privileges, and the abolition of serfdom. The guiding purpose of new state would be the "happiness and welfare of society in general and of each of its members in particular." There could be no other justification for obedience to the state and its laws.[26]

The Decembrists did not doubt the realism of their "audacious dreams." All of their experiences as educated and privileged men in a changing world convinced them of the necessity and inevitability of this new state and society. When government interrogators later asked that they explain how they came to be "infected" by dangerous liberal ideas, incarcerated Decembrists variously pointed to the lessons of Greek and Roman history, the modern history of revolutions (especially in France and America), books they read (mostly in French), witnessing the suffering of Russian serfs (most were from serf-owning families), and "the spirit of the age." Above all, they answered, new thinking was the natural result of thinking itself: "a liberal cast of mind took shape in me from the moment I began to think; natural reason strengthened it."[27]

However, these were still "dreams" in the sense we have been seeing throughout this book: the "forward dreaming" that is an awakening to the "truth" that the world as it exists is not enough, and need not be as it is.[28] Around 1820, the Decembrist Alexander Ulybyshev wrote a short story titled "A Dream." The author, a member of the "Green Lamp" literary society, a culturally radical group associated with Union of Welfare, prefaced his account with the reminder that dreams are "previews of our future" and have the power we need to "revive in one's heart hope that is almost dead." Dreams might be "illusions," but they usefully challenge "the real misfortunes with which our life is constantly surrounded."

Ulybyshev dreamed he was in St. Petersburg 300 years in the future, three centuries after a great revolution. Familiar government buildings, associated with oppression, had long since been given new purposes. A former royal palace was the "Palace of the State Assembly." Another palace was a Pantheon to individuals who had contributed to the new society. On the "ruins of fanaticism"—the site of a monastery—stood a triumphal arch. The revolution also constructed new buildings, such as a Rotunda of unprecedented "size and magnificence," but simple in design and without pictures or statues, as a Temple to the Creator. At the Temple of Justice, "any citizen at any time can demand protection of the law." In place of a standing army—defined as "idlers and thieves organized into regiments"—was the nation organized into a military reserve, and not to "uphold despotism" but only for defense. The main task of government was to ensure the people's "well-being": promoting agriculture, trade, and industry, and giving support to the dwindling numbers of the poor. The national symbol of the new Russian state was no longer "the two-headed eagle with lightning in its claws" but "a phoenix soaring into the sky and holding in its beak a wreath of olive branches and immortelles."[29]

"There Is Not and Cannot Ever Be a Good, Just, and Moral State"

Belief in the necessity and value of the state was shared widely across the political spectrum: by conservative ideologists of "orthodoxy, autocracy, and nationality"; progressive monarchs like Catherine the Great; liberals who believed in a progressive state standing "above classes" and parties in order to promote and protect democratic participation and the common good;[30] and, we shall see, Marxists, who believed that a revolutionary proletarian "dictatorship" was an essential path toward a classless and stateless future. Of course, these statists recognized that existing states all too often abused power and failed to act for the good. Hence their efforts to articulate the ideal new state.

Anarchists insisted that no state ruling from above, even a perfected state founded on virtue and union with the people, could be a force for positive change and a good society for all. Their idea of the "new state" was "no state," which is to say "no ruler" (*anarchon* in Greek). The very nature of the state is coercion, they insisted, and its main purpose is self-preservation. There can be no virtuous state. "The only virtuous state is a weak state," declared Mikhail Bakunin (the one-time Westernizer intellectual and now influential anarchist) in 1868.[31] This was more than a negative critique, more than a denunciation of the failings of every existing or imaginable state to lead societies toward the common good. Anarchism was based on a belief in the inevitable historical movement of humanity toward a free society that would allow every human being to realize their natural dignity and full potential.[32] The anarchist political ideal is a free, decentralized, self-regulating society, built and sustained from the bottom-up through the voluntary association of free and equal individuals. And this goal, they insisted, is based on reality not fantasy, on observation not wish nor desire. It is based on "the natural human need and desire for freedom" and the natural movement of history toward freedom.[33]

Bakunin found the contradictions between the world as it was and as it should be too unbearable to limit himself to philosophical contemplation or the work of writing and publishing, like his friends Alexander Herzen and Vissarion Belinsky. What he said of himself at the age of twenty, though he was not yet thinking about politics, can be extended to his later activist and anarchist personality. Writing to his parents in 1834 about feeling restricted and bored by the life of a military officer, he described his mind and spirit as "boiling," his desire to escape the "cold and unsurmountable obstacles of the physical world," his hope to find a more intense and active life. Recalling the idyllic home life he had left—a place of love, idealism, and possibility—he dreamed of "working for the future, on the foundation of memories of the past."[34] This is the psychological predisposition of the utopian: unable to accept the "darkness of the lived moment" as the only reality possible, and thus propelled to seek the "not-yet."[35] Leaving Russia in 1840 for Western Europe, Bakunin was drawn toward circles of active revolutionaries. Karl Marx impressed him for his sophisticated analysis of society, but he found his ideas about revolution and socialism overly authoritarian. Pierre Proudhon, the first to call himself an "anarchist," impressed Bakunin for his "far greater feeling for freedom" than Marx.[36] In 1845, writing from Paris, he assured his family that "I have not bowed before the so-called necessities of the real world and am their enemy as before and hope to defeat them." The principle inspiring his struggle against reality had also not changed: "unconditional faith in the proud greatness of the human being [*chelovek*], in his sacred calling, in freedom as the only source and only purpose of his life."[37]

A few years earlier, Bakunin had published in Germany a statement of his utopian determination to challenge "the so-called necessities of the real world." The German left, he argued, "exists only as the negation of reality as it is," "not yet" as an embodiment of "the fullness of life." As a result, the German left is "only the future and not yet the present." Negation is certainly necessary. But refusal to accept that the narrow reality of the present as the only possible reality is just a first step toward "a new, affirmative, organic reality." And signs of this new reality "are already stirring around us." The common people, especially, are rousing themselves and demanding that the rights granted to them only theoretically in European countries be granted in living reality.

Even Russians (he pretended to be a Frenchman writing in German) felt this rumbling new reality.

All nations and all people are filled with a kind of premonition . . . and look forward with trembling expectation to the approaching future, which will speak the redeeming word. Even in Russia, that endless snow-covered realm about which we know so little and which perhaps has a great future, even in Russia dark clouds are gathering, heralding a storm.

He challenged those who "compromised" with reality to "open their hearts to truth, to free themselves of their wretched and blind wisdom." And he challenged those embracing only negation to understand that "the passion for destruction is also a creative passion!"[38]

Negation, for Bakunin, was a call to action. Destruction was not only philosophical. The revolutions that broke out across Europe in 1848 drew him onto the streets and the barricades. Arrested in Dresden and sentenced to death, he was deported to Russia, where he was exiled to Siberia. In 1861, he escaped through Japan and America back to Europe, where he again threw himself into every possible opportunity for revolutionary action. In Italy, he worked with national liberation movements inspired by Mazzini and Garibaldi. In Switzerland, he joined Marx's International Workingmen's Association (the First International) but was expelled for his constant criticisms of Marxists and Marx himself. So, he established the Anarchist International. In Lyon, France, he helped lead a workers' uprising.

Bakunin's anarchist ideas developed during these years of action. In 1867, speaking at the First Congress of the League of Peace and Freedom in Geneva, he denounced all existing states, whether democratic republics or authoritarian monarchies, as incompatible with freedom, justice, and morality, indeed, as "the most flagrant, the most cynical, and the most complete negation of humanity."[39] The following year, at the second congress, he expanded on why it was necessary to "abolish the state—all states":

The state is force, oppression, exploitation, injustice elevated into a system that is the cornerstone of every society. The state has never possessed morality and never will. Its only morality and its only idea of justice is its own self-preservation and power—before which humanity must bow. The state is the complete negation of humanity.

To those at the congress who thought that existing states could be used to advance peace and freedom, he warned:

It is impossible to make the state change its nature . . . because then it would cease to exist. There is not and cannot ever be a good, just, and moral state. . . . . They are the diametrical opposite of human justice, freedom, and morality.[40]

The same would apply to a socialist state, he would later explain:

No state, no matter how democratic its form, not even the reddest political republic . . . can give the people what they need: free self-organization of their own affairs from the bottom up . . . without any interference, tutelage, or compulsion from above, because every state, even the pseudo-people's state concocted by Herr Marx, is in essence nothing other than a mechanism for ruling the masses from above, by means of a privileged minority of intellectuals, who imagine that they know what the people need and want better than do the people themselves.[41]

The Commune State: Dictatorship and Democracy

"Herr Marx," for his part, mocked the anarchist faith that the state could be abolished the moment workers took power. Of course, Marx sneered, we too look forward to a day without rulers, armies, police, or compulsion. But anarchists think that anything less than immediate abolition would be a sinful compromise with principles:

"As truly religious men they scorn daily needs and cry out with voices full of faith: 'May our class be crucified, may our race perish, but let the eternal principles remain immaculate!'" True revolutionaries, he insisted, know that a transitional "revolutionary dictatorship" is unavoidable.[42] Engels, always adept at popularizing Marx's arguments, developed the point:

> The anti-authoritarians demand that . . . the first act of the social revolution shall be the abolition of authority. Have these gentlemen ever seen a revolution? A revolution is certainly the most authoritarian thing there is; it is the act whereby one part of the population imposes its will upon the other part by means of rifles, bayonets and cannon?[43]

At the same time, Marx had earlier argued, revolutionaries cannot simply seize hold of and use the state that the old ruling class created in its own interests: the mistake of all past revolutions was trying to "perfect" the state "instead of breaking it."[44]

Lenin developed these arguments in *State and Revolution*, which he wrote in the summer of 1917.[45] As always, even when wandering deep in questions of history and theory, Lenin asked "what is to be done?"— as he had years before when borrowing this title of Chernyshevsky's vision of radical possibility for his own key political statement about reality and possibility. Like Marx, Lenin mocked the naïve utopianism of Russian anarchists, who were insisting that the revolution must immediately "abolish" the state. But even more strenuously, for they were more numerous and closer at hand, Lenin criticized Marxists who thought that the existing machinery of state could be adapted to the proletarian cause. No, Lenin insisted, the oppressed class cannot seize the "oppressive apparatus" of the state for its own purposes but must "destroy" the state that the old ruling class made to preserve its class power. This is "the chief and fundamental point in the Marxist theory of the state," Lenin argued, even though in "ninety-nine cases out of a hundred, if not more," most Marxists failed to understand this.

States are institutions of coercion, Lenin acknowledged. The state is "an organ for the repression of one class by another," which it does not only with force but also with a legal "order" that institutionalizes and legitimates repression. But unlike the anarchists, Marxists know that coercion will be required to suppress the opposition of the old ruling elites and to "abolish exploitation" and class difference. This is the only way, Lenin insisted, toward a future stateless society. Yes, this transitional state will be a coercive "dictatorship," but one founded on "democracy for the vast majority of the people" (including women, still excluded in most capitalist democracies) and "forceful suppression of the exploiters and oppressors of the people, i.e. their exclusion from democracy."

But this "revolutionary dictatorship" will also be a new type of state, a state that (Lenin quoted Engels here) will "no longer be a state in the proper sense of the word." The old state—based on coercive rule of a minority over the majority—would indeed be "abolished" in the revolution because now the majority exercises that rule. This new state will be a new type of state in other ways, too. When Marx and Engels were writing the *Communist Manifesto* in 1847, Lenin observed, they did not speculate on the new state that a revolution would bring, for "Marx did not indulge in utopias" but waited to see what would grow out of the "experience of the mass movement." Such experience manifested itself in the Paris Commune of 1871, revealing elements of the new state: an "armed people" replacing the standing army; officials elected and subject to immediate recall; police under the democratic control of the people; administrative tasks "simplified" such that any literate person could do the work; salaries of state officials reduced to the level of workers' wages to help undermine privilege and "grandeur"; parliamentary "talking shops" replaced by "working bodies" of elected deputies holding real power; the old administrative machine based on "bossing by bureaucrats" replaced by task-oriented managers and accountants. "We are not utopians . . .. We do not 'dream' of immediately going without any administration, without any subordination. These are anarchist dreams." But we can change the structure of subordination, giving power "to the armed vanguard of all the exploited and working people."[46]

Even this would be only a way station on the road to a society where "the capitalists have disappeared" and there is "no distinction between members of society in their relations to the social means of production" so no need for a coercive state. Lenin liked Engels's phrase about the state "withering away," "for it indicates that this is both a gradual and spontaneous process." "We are not utopians," he repeated: we recognize that some individuals will choose not to get along with others or to work for the good of all, mostly due to old "habits" that had not yet died out in changed conditions. But these will be individuals to suppress rather than an entire class, and so there will be no need for a "special apparatus of suppression," that is, a "state." And, with time, these individual "excesses" will "wither away." The only remaining "state" functions will be "accounting and oversight," not by a separate class of bureaucrats but "by everyone," "so that everyone may become a 'bureaucrat' for a time so that nobody may become a 'bureaucrat.'"

Within a few months of writing *State and Revolution*—unfinished because of the unexpected resurgence of revolution—Lenin was at the helm of a "revolutionary dictatorship." It has often been said that Lenin's approach to rule was contradictory at best and hypocritical at worst. But these contradictions can be seen, at least in part, as following the logic of Lenin's understanding of the Marxist theory of the new state. One the one hand, Lenin continued to talk of a new type of state inspired by the Paris Commune: instead of a parliament, real working power in the hands of "soviets" (councils) of elected worker, soldier, and peasant deputies, institutions that were products of "the creative enthusiasm" of the masses; local "workers' control" in enterprises; a de-bureaucratized "state apparatus of one million people" who serve not for "fat sums" but "for the sake of high ideals"; reducing inequality by distributing housing and other necessities to the needy; and, above all, "imbuing the oppressed and the working people with confidence in their own strength."[47] In the first months after coming to power, Lenin regularly appealed to "working people," as the "makers of history," to "remember that you yourselves are now administering the state." "Take matters into your own hands from below," he declared, "waiting for no one."[48] This was the realization of the "Commune State" (see Figure 8). Some historians have dismissed this talk as inauthentic in relation to the deeper ideology: as either temporary utilitarian expedients or a hypocritical way "to destroy the

Figure 8 V. I. Kozlinsky, "The Dead of the Paris Commune Resurrected Under the Red Banner of the Soviets." ROSTA Window Poster, 1920. © SPUTNIK / Alamy Stock Photo.

old political system and thus clear the way for the establishment of his own party's dictatorship."[49]

"Dictatorship," of course, even to the point of state terror, was openly embraced as a necessity and principle. Lenin continually reminded his comrades that Bolsheviks are "not anarchists," that Marxists know they must use the state's powers of discipline, coercion, and force. In practice, Bolsheviks did not hesitate to crush alleged enemies of proletarian power. The "fight for the new," Lenin argued in violent language, demanded "systematic coercion" against class enemies: "No mercy to these enemies of the people . . . . War to the death against the rich and their hangers-on, the bourgeois intellectuals, war against crooks, idlers, and hooligans," against "parasites." We must "cleanse the Russian land" of these "harmful insects."[50] Once the civil war was at full boil, Lenin demanded "merciless class terror" against the "kulaks [richer peasants], rich men, bloodsuckers" and every other enemy of the revolution.[51] This was more than a matter of necessity. It was virtue. A war to overcome the divisions of class that were the cause of violence, Lenin wrote, was the only war in history "that is legitimate, just, and sacred,"[52] the only path into a future without violence, without class inequalities, and without the state as it has been known through history. The end, he might have said, not only justifies any means necessary but ennobles the means.

"To Conduct Our Lives According to Our Own Will and Our Own Conception of Truth"

The Russian American anarchist Emma Goldman, after her "disillusionment" with the Russian revolution, commented that the "Russian people" are "to some extent instinctive Anarchists": untutored, naïve, and lacking a clear grasp of "libertarian principles," but feeling an "instinctive hatred of tyranny" and a natural desire for liberty, equality, and justice.[53] Less positively, Lenin agreed: in 1921, at the Tenth Party Congress, he warned of the threat posed by widespread "petty-bourgeois anarchistic *stikhiia*," a term usually translated as spontaneity but meaning the elements, the force of nature.[54] It is not for the historian to label these mentalities as instinctual or natural, but I too was struck, when reading hundreds of letters, proclamations, and other writings by workers, soldiers, and peasants during the revolution, by the intense and widespread desire for freedom and justice—and by the disillusionment with one government after another.[55] Of course, how people defined freedom and justice is a question.

Here is an example of one of these texts. Toward the end of March 1917, a worker and a deserter from the front wrote a letter to the new

Provisional Government mocking their promises of freedom as a "new lie" in a long history of lies by states: "The slogan of our era is 'Freedom!' 'Down with coercion!'" But this is a "foul lie." Men are still sent into war like "voiceless slaves" and "sheep." The elite and the state are still "parasites" that "ride on the backs of the people," squeezing every drop of life from them. "Do the people really want you to look after them, take care of them, etc? No, the people want you to get off their backs." That includes the state. "I am an enemy of state order no matter what it is . . . . Every state authority (even in democratic states) is founded on coercing its own subjects . . . . Where there is freedom, there cannot be coercion, and where there is coercion there cannot be freedom." Then he carefully added, "I am no anarchist. I am a proletarian free of prejudice."[56]

There were hundreds of similar statements by workers, peasants, and rank-and-file soldiers during those years, declaring freedom to be the most essential thing. But freedom was understood complexly. In part, it was a negative, libertarian ideal: the absence of coercive authority by elites: "get off the people's back." Voices of workers, peasants, and soldiers during the revolution are full of complaints about elites as usurpers, tyrants, traitors, plunderers, parasites, and "enemies of the people." But no less often, people saw "freedom" in affirmative terms: as bringing to the common people "a new life," a "good life," "happiness," "joy." And this meant not just talk but addressing concrete social needs: now that they were "free," many said, poverty and inequality must end, war must end, and life must get materially better.

These social benefits, it seemed to many, required the coercive power of the state. Before October, numerous appeals were sent to the leaders of the soviets, as nongovernmental representatives of the common people, to intervene in matters ranging from the local and particular (such as helping workers get rid of a cruel foreman or estate manager or a corrupt official); to ensure the people had food, land, and education; and to suppress "enemies" of the people's happiness, ranging from ordinary criminals taking advantage of disorder to large capitalists and landowners, whose very existence meant depriving the common people of happiness. Women looked to the new revolutionary state to grant them political and economic rights and defend these against male power and prejudice. Non-Russians looked to the new state to overcome the structures and legacies of empire and prejudice. Again and again, we hear calls for "firm authority" that could act rather than simply "talk." After October, these hopes were directed at the new Communist state.

Many personalized their vision of the new state by appealing to individuals, especially government and Soviet officials as trusted leaders and even as saviors who would bring the people happiness: "You are our Heroes strengthening our freedoms . . . . You are our friends, you are our saviors, and we trust you, and our hope is in you for the salvation of the working population of Russia."[57] This personalized view of political authority has been explained most often as the persistence of "a monarchic mentality." But more was involved here than simply the continuity of authoritarian tradition or a belief in strong power for its own sake. State power, and especially personalized power, was understood, as freedom was understood, as a source of justice, as a means to ensure the coming (in words so often heard here) of salvation, truth, justice, freedom, and "the kingdom of heaven on earth for the people." Needless to say, this hope could be a catalyst for disappointment.

During 1917, anarchists and Bolsheviks both claimed to be fighting for freedom and justice. Both fought for the same immediate goals: workers' control of factories, land to those who worked it, seizing the property of the rich, and the establishment of workers' and soldiers' councils from the bottom-up. Both opposed the "imperialist war" and refused to recognize the "bourgeois democratic" Provisional Government. Both were inspired by the Paris Commune of 1871. Both believed destruction of the old and suppression of enemies to be necessary to create the new and the free.

But the more the Bolsheviks talked about "dictatorship of the proletariat," the more suspicious anarchists grew. Before October, anarchists were already warning that "political organizations . . ., not excluding the Bolsheviks, entice the workers with the promise of the kingdom of god on earth hundreds of years from now." Workers must demand the new world now, they declared. And state power can never be the means to this end: only the "uprising of slaves" themselves can create the new world of equality.[58] In the first days and weeks of Soviet power, anarchist publications (before they were down) warned that "the action of parties is no substitute for social revolution" and that revolutionary state power will "inevitably strangle the revolution."[59] During the civil war, when the restoration of tsarism and all that went with it seemed possible, many anarchists fought to defend Soviet power against the Whites. Some formed independent detachments of partisans to fight the Whites while also pressing anarchist goals.

Perhaps the most famous of these anarchist warriors was the Ukrainian peasant leader Nestor Makhno. During the civil war, when Ukraine was occupied by a succession of different anti-Soviet forces (German, Austrian, Ukrainian, Whites, and others), Makhno established the Revolutionary Insurrectionary Army of Ukraine to fight against all of these enemies of the revolution. The goal, however, was "not to . . . hand over our fate to some new master, but to take it into our own hands and conduct our lives according to our own will and our own conception of truth."[60] Makhno's "Black Army" (as distinct from the Red and White armies, but also Russian peasant "Green Armies") opposed both "bourgeois-landlord authorities" and "the Bolshevik-Communist dictatorship." Its stated goal was to "liberate the working people of Ukraine from oppression," free localities of "all coercive organizations," and establish "a true soviet socialist order." For some of his troops, this also meant violently ridding Ukraine of Jews, though Makhno himself publicly criticized these pogroms. In January 1920, as victory over the Whites approached, the movement laid out its vision of the new order, to be carried out immediately: abolish all decrees by the White authorities but also all Communist decrees that "conflict with the interests" of workers and peasants; transfer all lands into the hands of those who personally work the land; transfer all industrial enterprises to workers through their trade unions; create new soviets without the participation of political parties; abolish all militias, police, armies, Chekas [Bolshevik political police], party revolutionary committees, and "similar coercive, authoritarian, and disciplinarian institutions"; and give responsibility for social order and safety to worker-peasant self-defense units.[61] In June, the movement issued an appeal to Red Army soldiers who had been sent to crush the Makhno army:

> We revolutionary insurgents and Makhnovists are also peasants and workers . . . fighting for a better and brighter life. . . . Our ideal is a toilers' community without rulers, without parasites, without commissar-bureaucrats. Our immediate aim is the establishment of a free soviet order without the power of the Bolsheviks, without compulsion by any party . . . . Think about it. Whose side are you on? Don't be a slave—be a man [*chelovek*]![62]

People's Power

The civil war left Soviet power facing a collapsed economy, epidemics, urban depopulation, a flood of refugees, millions of unsupervised and homeless children, rural banditry, urban crime, peasant rebellions, and workers' protests (mainly economic but mixed with anger at the privileges of party elites and increasingly coercive management). Soviet Russia was deep in a dystopian darkness only partly of its own making. Historians have spoken of the psychological and physical condition of Soviet Russia at the end of the civil war as that of "trauma."[63] Lenin admitted after seven years of war that Russia was like a "man beaten to within an inch of his life."[64] On top of material catastrophe, the party leadership worried about the dangerous "mood" of the masses of peasants and even workers. There was reason to doubt whether the victorious Bolshevik state would be able to survive this profound social and economic crisis.

And then, in early March 1921, sailors, soldiers, and workers at the Kronstadt naval base outside of Petrograd rebelled against the state they had helped to bring into being. In 1917, Lev Trotsky had acclaimed "Red Kronstadt" to be "the pride and glory of the revolution."[65] Now, Red Kronstadt demanded free elections to new soviets, since "the present soviets do not express the will of workers and peasants," freedom of speech and press "for workers and peasants, anarchists, and left socialist parties," freedom for socialist political prisoners, an end to the Communist Party's "special privileges for propagating its ideas," an end to surveillance and control in factories by armed Communists, and giving peasants "full rights to action on their own land" as long as they do not hire labor.[66] Anarchists hailed the Kronstadt uprising as a "second Paris Commune."[67] While some of the sailors and the leaders of the revolt may have identified as anarchists, most thought of themselves as communists. They were convinced they represented the true spirit of October: a free working peoples' republic where power grows from below. The October Revolution, they declared, gave workers "hope" for "emancipation," but brought "even greater enslavement of the human personality [*lichnost*]." Communists had appropriated the "power of the police-gendarme monarchy," so that, instead of freedom, the people got "bayonets, bullets, and rude commands." Worst of all was the "moral servitude": Communist authorities have "laid their hands on the inner world of working people to force people to think only as they do." All that matters to the new state is to preserve its power and it will use "slander, violence, deceit, and murder" to achieve it.[68] "Power to the soviets, not to the parties," they declared. The "party dictatorship" did not represent the people's will but had become a body of "parasites, living at the expense of the toiling masses." This would happen with any party in power, no matter their ideology, for the liberated political order must be worked out "in the cauldron of life" by the people themselves, not "behind office walls" by "party wise men."[69]

This dangerous challenge was paralleled by dissent within the Communist Party itself. In 1920, several Bolshevik trade union leaders had organized a "Workers' Opposition" to oppose traditional forms of discipline in factories, the use of "bourgeois specialists" as engineers and managers, and the subordination of trade unions to the state.[70] Activists warned that "you cannot build a planned economy the way the pharaohs built their pyramids."[71] They demanded "control" of the economy by trade unions and other workers' institutions, power within unions in the hands of rank-and-file workers, and the restoration of democratic elections and freedom of discussion within the ruling party. They declared their enemy to be the "enormous bureaucratic machine" that was growing at the expense of "the creative initiative and self-activity" of organized workers, who alone could overcome economic ruin and build a socialist society.[72]

In preparation for the Tenth Party Congress in March 1921, the Workers' Opposition issued a pamphlet laying out their positions, written by Alexandra Kollontai. Lenin and Trotsky criticized them for making a "fetish of democratic principles" and preferring fantasy to reality.[73] In turn, the Workers' Opposition claimed a richer sense of reality and possibility. They mocked the "sober" policies of state and party leaders, the "state wisdom . . . of our ruling heights," their supposedly sensible willingness to "adapt" and "compromise." "Today we might gain something with the help of your 'sober policy,'" Kollontai imagined workers saying to the party establishment, "but let us beware lest we find ourselves on a false road that, through turns and zigzags, will imperceptibly lead us away from the future toward the debris of the past."[74] The only way to open the world of "new possibilities," the only path for "the creation of new forms of production and life," is "freedom" for workers to "speak their creative new word." The party leadership, unfortunately, "distrusted" the very workers who ought to be the foundation of the "proletarian dictatorship." And this distrust produced two evils: "bureaucracy," which is the "direct negation of mass self-activity," and workers' growing "bitterness" and "alienation" from the government, which further "deadens and kills the self-activity of the masses."[75]

The new communist state must be radically different from the traditional state. It must be built and powered from the bottom-up. "It is impossible to decree communism. It can be created only through the lived experiences and desires and creative effort of the working class itself, even if they are sometimes mistaken." Against Trotsky's argument that the problem is not bureaucracy itself but a tendency to adopt the "bad sides of bureaucratism," the Workers' Opposition answered that there are no good sides to bureaucracy. It is an unambiguous "scourge," which "has seeped into the very marrow of our party and eaten through to soviet institutions." Bureaucracy treats "every new thought" as "heresy" and replaces the open exchange of opinions and initiative from below with "decisions handed down from above." The sooner the party leadership understands these errors and these truths, "the sooner we can step across that forbidden border beyond which humanity, freed from external economic laws and with the rich and valuable knowledge of collective experience, will begin consciously to create the history of humanity in the communist epoch"—the sooner, Kollontai might have added, that humanity can "leap from the kingdom of necessity to the kingdom of freedom."[76] This leap is impossible, even many Communist critics of the growing Communist state worried, when there is only "state wisdom."

"We Are Bound by No Laws. There Are No Fortresses That Bolsheviks Cannot Storm"

At the end of the 1920s, the Soviet state suddenly and dramatically turned away from the sober, reasoned, statecraft that defined the New Economy Policy, which was the party's carefully calibrated answer to the terrible crisis at the end of the civil war. NEP offered concessions to peasant demands and tolerance of small private business on order to restore social peace and enable the economy to recover. At the same time, to strengthen political order, there was a complete ban on dissident groups within the ruling Communist Party and growing control over public political and cultural debate. NEP was a "retreat" from both creative destruction of the old and radical experiments with the new. Economically, it was a turn toward the slow and steady building of socialism through market mechanisms combined with state control of large-scale industry. Nikolai Bukharin, a party leader and advocate of NEP, described this in 1925 as the need "for a long time yet [to] ride on a skinny peasant horse" toward socialism.[77] This was far from the heroic revolutionism many longed for.

After defeating all other contenders for power following Lenin's death in 1924, including Trotsky on the left (favoring state-driven industrialization) and Bukharin on the right (insisting on slow and balanced growth), Joseph Stalin launched a campaign of rapid industrialization, mass collectivization of agriculture, and class war against old elites and old ideas in every field of public life, from economics to education. A suitable slogan for this "Great Turn" was Stalin's repeated declaration that "there are no fortresses that Bolsheviks cannot storm," that it is possible to achieve levels of economic growth "about which we now do not even dare to dream."[78] He borrowed the metaphor from an economist, who went even further: "Our task is not to study economics but to change it. We are bound by no laws. There are no fortresses that Bolsheviks cannot storm."[79] This "revolution from above," as many historians have called it, was not only from above. Stalin understood that one cannot simply "decree communism." This required mass mobilization and participation. In part, this campaign of mass participation was an example of what the Kronstadt rebels called the "moral servitude" of "forcing people to think only as they do." But it was never so simple: Soviet citizens learned to "act Bolshevik" and "speak Bolshevik" in ways that were variously coerced (fearing punishment for failure), performative (*as if* one believed), and internalized (defining one's self through Soviet values and collective belonging).[80]

Stalin's First Five-Year Plan (1928–32), the heart of the Great Turn, was less a "plan" in any normal sense of the word than a call to heroic revolutionary action and belief. Production targets were set at absurdly high levels and then raised to higher ones. And even though targets were already unrealistic for five years, it was proclaimed that they would be reached and exceeded in four years. "Five-in-Four," and sometimes "Two Plus Two Equals Five," became slogans of this movement—the latter taken up by George Orwell in *Nineteen Eighty-Four* as a metaphor for dystopian unreason and thought control.[81] Soviet propagandists, however, had an answer to those who mocked their utopian arithmetic and seeming faith in miracles: just add "the enthusiasm of the workers" and the formula was complete and realistic (see Figure 9).

Struggling to leap free of the slow and steady march of time was an obsession during the Stalin Revolution, as it has been in most utopian thinking. "We are behind the advanced countries by 50-100 years," Stalin told a meeting of industrial managers in February 1931. "We must race across that distance in ten years."[82] Journalism, literature,

Figure 9 Ia. Guminer, "Arithmetic for Meeting the Plan: Two Plus Two (Plus the Enthusiasm of the Workers) Equals Five," 1931 Poster. © Heritage Images / Getty Images.

and film echoed and amplified these themes, as when the collectively written *People of the Stalingrad Tractor Factory* declared that in one year "we have advanced 200 years." Others wrote of "leaping" from the sixteenth century to the twentieth.[83] In such leaps across time, everything was to become "new" and "reborn," including the human individual. In practice, the plan succeeded in stimulating industrial development, rapid if unbalanced, but at great human cost. The utopian fight against the limits of possibility, especially combined with statist faith in "the civilizing role of force exerted from above," can produce its own dystopian leap, into a new darkness.

CONCLUSION

When I was in college, one of my teachers, a recent émigré from the Soviet Union, tried to explain to me what made Soviet "dissidents" resist the norms of a system that was so total in its desire to control people's lives that it was called "totalitarian." Of course, dissenters did not have the power to overcome the controlling and coercive machinery of a state that ruled not merely from above but from all sides of an individual's life. So they worked around the edges and in the interstices. This meant, most often, carefully nurtured spaces with trusted friends where power could not easily reach: places of honesty, authenticity, sincerity, and friendship—key values in these liberated zones of unofficial life. "We decided to live *as if* we were free," he told me. A modest yet bold orientation, which we can find in many different historical situations. The Czechoslovak dissident Václav Havel famously called this "living in truth" and viewed it as "power" for the "powerless."[1]

Throughout this book we have seen men and women try to imagine and live as "new people" in the old present, even if the new society remained only a distant dream, an improbable possibility. This was what Nikolai Chernyshevsky meant when he called on people to "bring what you can from the future into the present." And this is the practice of critical life we have seen across modern Russian history. However differently, believers and atheists, conservatives and revolutionaries, communists and anti-communists found "the vile fetters of reality" (to recall Vissarion Belinsky's phrase) unjustifiable and unbearable. And if the "vile" present was too strong to overturn, people found ways to live apart and against it, to disrupt its reach, to interrupt its power.

A crucial disruption, we have seen, was to think about time differently, as uneven and nonlinear: to reclaim and rework a lost past to create a new future, to "leap" through time and space toward the kingdom of freedom, to fly on "the fiery wings of time." Walter Benjamin's notion that there are "splinters of messianic time" always present in the here and now was an effort to theorize this alternative temporality of possibility. Russian history has been rich in stories of people bringing a dreamed future into the dark present, disrupting the steady stream of the seemingly unchangeable, breaking the fetters of reality. Russia, of course, has been neither alone nor unique in such stories.

Nothing is certain when one "ventures beyond" the known and the familiar, when one takes a daring "leap in the open air" of historical possibility.[2] To leap into the space of freedom is full of risk and chance. There are no guarantees. Thinking about the Russian revolution when revising in 1923 his book *Spirit of Utopia*, Ernst Bloch concluded that "doors opened; but, of course, they soon shut."[3] I have interpreted the history of Russian Utopia as full of potential, open to many roads, with many doors. It is common, and a mistake, to judge what matters in history by reading history backward from outcomes. We must resist this tyranny of outcomes. We cannot know what was only unrealized rather than unrealistic. Of course, it would be naïve to think that every dream of new possibility is really possible. It would be no less naïve to ignore histories of failure, the inability to overcome the darkness of lived reality, and all too many cases when idealism produced terrible darkness and brutality—the dystopia that is utopia's troubling twin. Still, we must take seriously the persistence of human refusal, again and again in history, to bow down to the supposed wisdom of accepting what *is* as the only reality.

Utopia, to carry this further, need not be realistic to be historically powerful and meaningful. Utopia, we have argued, is a critical method, a declaration that the present is not enough, that "something is missing." Utopia interrupts the complacency and pessimism of the here and now. It cannot be satisfied. If true to itself, it is always bringing the future into the present, always unrealized, challenging the inadequacies of every present. Perhaps, the future can never be now, and utopia can never be a place. It must always be somewhere else, a constant reminder that something is *still* missing. In this way, I see the Russian utopias in this book, and others I might have told of, not as gravestones along the path of failed or distorted dreams but as examples of the human impulse to grasp the "splinters of messianic time," to think and act critically in relation to the world as it is, to question assumptions, to "penetrate the darkness," "summon what is not," and "build ourselves into the blue" where "truth" is not held back by "the merely factual." Put differently, recalling metaphors we have seen before, utopia is the leap not the landing, the venturing beyond not the arrival, winged flight in the open air of possibility not entry into the kingdom of heaven.[4]

It is not surprising that so many have reached for metaphors in utopian thinking. We turn to metaphors when plain realism is not enough to understand the complexity of human experience and explore the realm of possibility. Metaphors are themselves "conceptual leaps."[5] Dreams, a leitmotif in this book, are a type of metaphor. In the nineteenth century, the Russian populist Gleb Uspensky recorded a hallucination during his mental illness: that he could fly and that the sight of him soaring above the world would overcome the oppressors with shame and inspire the oppressed with hope, bringing about God's Kingdom on Earth.[6] This is the utopian impulse: dreams, inspired by a bit of madness, that are a critical rethinking of reality, necessity, and possibility. Like dreams, utopia is a vision that "interrupts" and "surprises" reality rather than merely "explains" it.[7]

Thinking of utopia as hopeful interruption, I will conclude with one more metaphor, from a part of Walter Benjamin's theses on history that he set aside, perhaps because he was unsure how it fit into his scheme. For good measure, he couched this thought in the "perhaps" that is necessary for every utopia:

Marx says that revolutions are the locomotive of world history. But perhaps it is quite otherwise. Perhaps revolutions are an attempt by the passengers on this train—namely the human race—to activate the emergency brake.[8]

. . . and open the door, leap off, and venture into the open air, if only for a moment. Perhaps we should look toward "the unforeseeable and unpredictable" "miracle" that even Hannah Arendt, for all her world-weary gaze on twentieth-century history, knew to be natural and right for humanity to expect.[9] I would like to think that the men and women whose dreams are woven through this book would find these definitions of utopia a fair description of their thoughts, feelings, and work.

NOTES

Acknowledgments

1   Arundhati Roy, "The Pandemic Is a Portal," *Financial Times,* April 3, 2020, online https://www.ft.com/content/10d8f5e8-74eb-11ea-95fe-fcd2 74e920ca.

2   *New York Times*, June 4, 2020, Section A, page 1, online https://www.nyt imes.com/2020/06/03/us/politics/esper-milley-trump-protest.html?a ction=click&module=RelatedLinks&pgtype=Article

3   *The New York Times,* July 5, 2020, A:1, online https://www.nytimes.com /2020/07/04/us/politics/trump-mt-rushmore.html

4   Nikita Mitchell, "'We Are on the Cusp of Something Great': A Black Liberation Organizer on Next Steps for the Movement: An interview with Nikita Mitchell," *In These Times,* July 27, 2020, online https://in thesetimes.com/article/nikita-mitchell-interview-black-liberation-geor ge-floyd-protests-next-steps

5   See the Introduction.

Introduction

1   On dreams and utopia, see Ernst Bloch, *Geist der Utopie* (Munich and Leipzig: Duncker & Humblot, 1918; second ed., Berlin: Paul Cassirer, 1923), trans. Anthony Nassar as *The Spirit of Utopia* (Stanford: Stanford University Press, 2000), esp. 82, 144, 237 (quote); idem., *The Principle of Hope,* 3 vols. (Cambridge, MA: MIT Press, 1986–1995; written 1938–1947, first published in German in 1959), I:3–42; Walter Benjamin, *The Arcades Project*, trans. Howard Eiland and Kevin McLaughlin (Cambridge, MA: Harvard University Press, 1999), 463–4; Benjamin, "Dream Kitsch" (1927), "Experience and Poverty" (1935), "The Storyteller" (1936), in *Selected Writings,* 4 vols. (Cambridge, MA: Harvard University Press, 1996–2003), II:3–5, 731–6, III: 143–66. See

also Susan Buck-Morss, *Dreamworld and Catastrophe: The Passing of Mass Utopia in East and West* (Cambridge, MA: MIT Press, 2000); Eli Friedlander, *Walter Benjamin: A Philosophical Portrait* (Cambridge, MA: Harvard University Press, 2012), chap. 5 ("Dream").

2 In addition to *Spirit of Utopia* and *Principle of Hope*, see Ernst Bloch, *The Utopian Function of Art and Literature: Selected Essays*, trans. Jack Zipes and Frank Mecklenburg (Cambridge, MA: MIT Press, 1988). Among those who have elaborated on Bloch's approach to utopia, see especially Fredric Jameson, Ruth Levitas, and José Esteban Muñoz. For recent examples of historical work adapting this approach, see Maria Todorova, *The Lost World of Socialists at Europe's Margins: Imagining Utopia, 1870s-1920s* (London: Bloomsbury, 2020) and Faith Hillis, *Utopia's Discontents: Russian Exiles and the Quest for Freedom, 1830–1930* (New York: Oxford University Press, 2021). See "Selected Further Readings."

3 Bloch, *Principle of Hope*, 4–5, 12.

4 Bloch, *Spirit of Utopia*, 237.

5 Bloch, *Geist der Utopie*, 9.

6 "Something's Missing: A Discussion between Ernst Bloch and Theodor W. Adorno on the Contradictions of Utopian Longing" (1964), in Bloch, *The Utopian Function of Art and Literature*, 1–17.

7 See Andrzej Walicki, *Marxism and the Leap to the Kingdom of Freedom: The Rise and Fall of the Communist Utopia* (Stanford: Stanford University Press, 1995).

8 Benjamin, "On the Concept of History," *Selected Writings*, 4:389–411.

9 See "Selected Further Readings," especially historians Igal Halfin, Jochen Hellbeck, Faith Hillis, Aileen Kelly, John Randolph, Bernice Rosenthal, Yuri Slezkine, Richard Stites, Maria Todorova, and Andy Willimott, and scholars of literature and film Amindita Banerjee, Rolf Hellebust, Nina Gurianova, Lilya Kaganovsky, Catriona Kelly, and Olga Matich.

10 Michael D. Gordin, Helen Tilley, and Gyan Prakash, eds., *Utopia/Dystopia: Conditions of Historical Possibility* (Princeton: Princeton University Press, 2010), 2–3. Related, Yuri Slezkine has described the "apocalyptic millenarianism" that animated Bolshevism, which he defined as a modern "millenarian sect," as "the vengeful fantasy of the dispossessed, the hope for a great awakening in the midst of a great disappointment." Yuri Slezkine, *The House of Government: A Saga of the Russian Revolution* (Princeton: Princeton University Press, 2017), 99.

Chapter 1

1   On the first anniversary festival, held on November 7 because Russia leaped ahead in time when the new government adopted the Gregorian calendar used in the West, see James von Geldern, *Bolshevik Festivals, 1917-1920* (Berkeley: University of California Press, 1993).

2   Soldiers' resolutions printed in the Soviet newspaper *Izvestiia*, November 2, 21, and 30, 1917.

3   The viewpoint of the liberal newspaper *Rech'*, October 26, 1917.

4   From reports in the progressive newspaper *Gazeta dlia vsekh* between November 1917 and June 1918, when the paper was closed by the government.

5   M. Gerasimov, S. Esenin, and S. Klychkov, "Kantata," *Zarevo zavodov*, no. 1 (January 1919): 24–5.

6   S. T. Konenkov, *Moi vek* (Moscow: Politizdat, 1972), 222–3.

7   M., "Memorial'naia doska na Krasnoi ploshchadi," *Tvorchestvo*, no. 7 (November 1918): 26–7.

8   See Mikhail Guerman, *Art of the October Revolution* (Leningrad: Avrora, 1979).

9   For example, see the famous depiction of the French "Declaration of the Rights of Man and of the Citizen" of 1789 as painted by Le Barbier and the "Apotheosis of George Washington" in the eye of the rotunda of the US Capitol painted by Brumidi in 1865. For a socialist adaptation, see the cartoons of the British designer Walter Crane, such as "Labour's May Day," *c.* 1890.

10   See the Introduction.

11   On the influence of Nietzsche in Russia, see the writings and edited collections by Bernice Glatzer Rosenthal, especially her monograph, *New Myth, New World.* On Nietzsche's influence on Konenkov, see Rosenthal, "The Mystical Ambience," in Marie Lampard, John Bowlt, and Wendy Salmond, eds., *The Uncommon Vision of Sergei Konenkov* (New Brunswick: Rutgers University Press, 2001), 151.

12   Friedrich Nietzsche, *Thus Spoke Zarathustra*, trans. Walter Kaufmann (New York: Viking Press, 1966), 192.

13   See Mark D. Steinberg, *Proletarian Imagination: Self, Modernity, and the Sacred in Russia, 1910-1925* (Ithaca: Cornell University Press, 2002).

14   I. Eroshin, "Detstvo," *Tvorchestvo*, no. 4 (August 1918): 10–11.

15 M. Chernysheva, "Daite mne kryl'ia!" *Dumy narodnye*, no. 3 (February 13, 1910): 5.

16 A. Bibik, *K shirokoi doroge (Ignat iz Novoselovki)* (St. Petersburg, 1914), 71. The novel first appeared in the journal *Sovremennyi mir* in 1912.

17 I. Dozorov [Gastev], "My Idem!" *Metallist*, 1914, no. 1/38 (January 13): 3–4.

18 Maksim Gor'kii, "Chelovek," *Sbornik tovarishchestva 'Znanie' za 1903: kniga pervaia* (St. Petersburg: Znanie, 1904), online at http://gorkiy-lit .ru/gorkiy/proza/rasskaz/chelovek.htm. See also Chapter 2.

19 Maksim Gor'kii, "Ispoved'," in *Sbornik tovarishchestva "Znanie": kniga dvadtsat'* (St. Petersburg: Znanie, 1908), at http://gorkiy-lit.ru/gorkiy/pr oza/ispoved/ispoved-12.htm.

20 Petr Oreshin, "In the Fields," May 28, 1917, *Delo naroda*, no. 60 (May 28, 1917): 2.

21 Petr Oreshin, "Blagoslovi," *Rabochii mir*, 1918, no. 15 (October 13): 3.

22 V. Aleksandrovskii, "Krylia," *Gorn*, no. 5 (1920): 7–9 (read in 1919 at a Sunday meeting at the Proletcult literary studio in Moscow, *Gudki*, no. 5 [May 1919]: 28).

23 I. Sadof'ev, "Chto takoe proletkul't," *Mir i chelovek* (Kolpino), no. 1 (January 1919): 12.

24 See, for example, I. Sadof'ev, "Ognennyi put'," *Mir i chelovek*, no. 1 (January 1919): 4; and the entire collection *Zavod ognekrylyi* published in Moscow in 1918 by the Proletcult.

25 M. Gerasimov, "Letim," *Zavod ognekrylyi*, 17.

26 George Young, *The Russian Cosmists: The Esoteric Futurism of Nikolai Fedorov and His Followers* (Oxford: Oxford University Press, 2013); Boris Groys, ed. *Russian Cosmism* (Cambridge, MA: MIT Press, 2018).

27 A. Bogdanov, *Krasnaia zvezda: Roman-utopiia* (St. Petersburg: T-vo khudozhestvennoi pechati, 1908); Alexander Bogdanov, *Red Star: The First Bolshevik Utopia*, ed. Loren R. Graham and Richard Stites, trans. Charles Rougle (Bloomington: Indiana University Press, 1984). I used this translation, checked and sometimes adjusted with the Russian edition, as reprinted in A. A. Bogdanov, *Voprosy sotsializma: raboty raznykh let* (Moscow: Izd. Polit. literatury, 1990).

28 Pchela, "Kul't razvrata," *Peterburgskii listok*, December 8, 1908, 2. See also Mark Steinberg, *Petersburg Fin de Siècle* (New Haven: Yale University Press, 2011), chapter 7.

29 Bogdanov, *Red Star*, 42.

30 Ibid., 38.

31 Ibid., 47—translation adjusted based on Bogdanov, *Voprosy sotsializma*, 125.

32 See Scott Palmer, *Dictatorship of the Air: Aviation Culture and the Fate of Modern Russia* (Cambridge: Cambridge University Press, 2006); Vlad Strukov and Helena Goscilo, eds., *Russian Aviation, Space Flight, and Visual Culture* (London: Routledge, 2017).

33 Palmer, *Dictatorship of the Air*, 154.

34 In the artist's 1971 memoir, he says that the plaque remained on the Kremlin tower until 1948 when it was removed for preservation and a replacement copy made, though this was not installed. Konenkov, *Moi Vek*, 222–3.

35 B. Arvatov, "Oveshchestvlennaia utopia," *Lef: Zhurnal levoga fronta iskusstv*, no. 1 (March 1923): 61–4.

36 Eugene Lyons, *Assignment in Utopia* (New York: Harcourt, Brace and Company, 1937), 606.

37 "Chelovek" (1916–17), in V. V. Maiakovskii, *Izbrannye sochineniia v dvukh tomakh* (Moscow: Khudozhestvennaia literatura, 1981), vol. 2: 80–105.

38 "Revoliutsiia: poetokhronika" (April 17, 1917), Maiakovskii, *Izbrannye sochineniia* 1:95–101.

39 V. V. Maiakovskii, *Letaiushchii proletarii* (Moscow, 1925), in *Pol'noe sobranie sochinenii* (Moscow: Khudozhestvennaia literatura, 1955–61), vol. 6, online http://feb-web.ru/feb/mayakovsky/texts/ms0/ms6/ms6-311-.htm.

40 "Dorogu krylatomu Erosu! (Pis'mo k trudiashcheisia molodezhi)," *Molodaia gvardia*, 1923, no. 3 (May): 111–24, online http://az.lib.ru/k /kollontaj_a_m/text_0030.shtml. For a translation, see "Make Way for Winged Eros (A Letter to Working Youth)," in Alix Holt, ed., *Selected Writings of Alexandra Kollontai* (New York: W. W. Norton, 1977), 276–92.

41 Mikhail Kuzmin, *Kryl'ia*, originally published in the magazine *Vesy* in 1906. Quotations are from the Russian edition published in M. A. Kuzmin, *Proza i esseistika*, 3 vols. (Moscow: Agraf, 2014), vol. 1 (*Proza, 1906-1912*), 6–72. For a recent English translation, see Mikhail Kuzmin, *Wings*, trans. Hugh Aplin (London: Hesperus, 2007).

42 Kuzmin, *Kryl'ia*, 13.

43 Ibid., 25.

Notes

44 Ibid., 18.

45 Ibid., 71.

46 Ibid., 72.

47 John E. Malmstad, "Bathhouses, Hustlers, and a Sex Club: The Reception of Mikhail Kuzmin's *Wings*," *Journal of the History of Sexuality*, 9:1–2 (January–April 2000): 85–104.

Chapter 2

1 English translations of many of the works I discuss use "man" in instances where I use "human" or "person," or even humanity. Although "man" was once conventional in English as the generic for human being, we need not impose gendered language on Russian thought when it was not there. On occasion, I will use "Man," capitalized, especially when the individuals or works discussed were thinking in gendered terms.

2 Vladimir Dal', *Tolkovyi slovar' zhivogo velikorusskogo iazyka* (St. Petersburg: Izdanie M. O. Vol'fa, 1880–1), 4:588; D. N. Ushakov, ed., *Tolkovyi slovar' russkogo iazyka* (Moscow: Sovetskaia entsiklopediia, 1935–40), 4:1247.

3 Joseph Frank, *Dostoevsky: The Stir of Liberation, 1860-1865* (Princeton: Princeton University Press, 1986), 285, quoted in Michael R. Katz and William G. Wagner, "Introduction" to Nikolai Chernyshevsky, *What Is to Be Done?* trans. Michael R. Katz (Ithaca: Cornell University Press, 1989), 23.

4 G. V. Plekhanov in *Sotsial-demokrat* 1890, No. 1, in G. V. Plekhanov, *Izbrannye filosofskie proizvedeniia v piati tomakh*, vol. 4 (Moscow: Gos. izd. politicheskoi literatury, 1958), 159–60.

5 N. Valentinov, "Chernyshevskii i Lenin," *Novyi zhurnal* 26 (1951): 194.

6 Irina Paperno, *Chernyshevsky and the Age of Realism* (Stanford: Stanford University Press, 1988), 195–6, 217, 222.

7 Chernyshevsky, *What Is to Be Done?* 148; N. G. Chernyshevskii, *Chto delat'? Iz rasskazov o novykh liudiakh*, eds. T. I. Ornatskaia and S. A. Reiser (Leningrad: Nauka, 1975), chap. 2, part XVIII. Quotations are from Katz's excellent translation or slightly revised from the Russian. Citations list pages in the translation, followed by the chapter and section numbers of the Russian original.

8   See the discussion of the moral and religious meanings of these characters in Paperno, *Chernyshevsky*. For key discussions of Rakhmetov, see Chernyshevsky, *What Is to Be Done?* 291–3, 311–13 (3:XXIX, XXXI).

9   Chernyshevsky, *What Is to Be Done?* 443–5 (5:XXIII, 6).

10 See the Introduction.

11 Chernyshevsky, *What Is to Be Done?* 129–31 (2:XII).

12 Ibid., 180–8 (3:III).

13 Ibid., 380 (4:XVII).

14 Ibid., 236–43 (3:XIX).

15 P. F. Kudrina [P. F. Kudelli], "Natashiny sny (Rasskaz)," *Rabotnitsa*, no. 1 (February 23, 1914): 11–15.

16 Among many studies, see Remy Debes, ed., *Dignity: A History* (Oxford: Oxford University Press, 2017).

17 Andrzej Walicki, *A History of Russian Thought from the Enlightenment to Marxism* (Stanford: Stanford University Press, 1979), 16.

18 Douglas Smith, *Working the Rough Stone: Freemasonry and Society in Eighteenth-Century Russia* (DeKalb: Northern Illinois University Press, 1999); Raffaela Faggionato, *A Rosicrucian Utopia in Eighteenth-Century Russia: The Masonic Circle of N.I. Novikov* (Dordrecht: Springer, 2005), 1–5, 33, 67–8, 80, 82, 86–9, 141, 240; Tatiana Artemyeva, "Utopian Spaces of Russian Masons," in Andreas Önnerfors and Robert Collis, *Freemasonry and Fraternalism in Eighteenth-Century Russia* (Sheffield: Centre for Research, 2009), 63–84.

19 N. I. Novikov, "O vysokom chelovecheskom dostoianii," *Izbrannye proizvodennye* (Moscow: Khudozhestvennaia literatura, 1951), 381–7.

20 Alexander Herzen, *My Past and Thoughts*, trans. Constance Garnett (New York: Knopf, 1974), 245.

21 Herzen, *My Past and Thoughts*, 292–4.

22 Andrzej Walicki, *The Slavophile Controversy: History of a Conservative Utopia in Nineteenth-Century Russian Thought* (Oxford: Oxford University Press, 1967); Walicki, *History of Russian Thought*, chap. 6; Susanna Rabow-Edling, *Slavophile Thought and the Politics of Cultural Nationalism* (Albany: SUNY Press, 2012).

23 Rabow-Edling, *Slavophile Thought*; Herzen, *My Past and Thoughts*; Isaiah Berlin, *Russian Thinkers*, ed. Henry Hardy and Aileen Kelly (Harmondsworth: Penguin, 1978), esp. 114–209; Aileen Kelly, *Toward*

Notes

Another Shore: Russian Thinkers between Necessity and Chance (New Haven: Yale University Press, 1998); Aileen Kelly, *The Discovery of Chance: The Life and Thought of Alexander Herzen* (Cambridge, MA: Harvard University Press, 2016); Walicki, *A History of Russian Social Thought*, chaps. 7–10.

24 V. Belinskii, "Pis'mo k N. V. Gogoliu," 15 July 1847, in V. G. Belinskii, *Polnoe sobranie sochinenii* vol. 10 (Moscow: Izd. Akademiia Nauk, 1956), 212–14.

25 Letter to V. P. Botkin, March 1, 1841, in V. G. Belinskii, *Sobranie sochinenii v deviati tomakh*, vol. 9 (Moscow: Khudozestvennaia literatura, 1982), 445.

26 Letters to Botkin, January 15, March 1, September 8, 1841, *Polnoe sobranie sochinenii*, vol. 9: 431–4, 442–50, 478–86.

27 Ibid., September 8, 1841.

28 See John W. Randolph, *The House in the Garden: The Bakunin Family and the Romance of Russian Idealism* (Ithaca: Cornell University Press, 2007).

29 Richard Stites, *The Women's Liberation Movement in Russia* (Princeton: Princeton University Press, 1978), 17–25; Barbara Engel, *Mothers and Daughters: Women of the Intelligentsia in Nineteenth-Century Russia* (Cambridge: Cambridge University Press, 1983), chaps. 1–2.

30 Maria Ogareva, quoted in Engel, *Mothers and Daughters*, 28.

31 Engel, *Mothers and Daughters*, 3.

32 S[ergei] Stepniak[-Kravchinskii], *Underground Russia: Revolutionary Profiles and Sketches from Life*, translated from the Italian (New York: Scribner's Sons, 1882), 4. I have corrected the translation with the Russian text, online at http://www.lib.ru/PRIKL/STEPNYAK/podpol.txt.

33 Engel, *Mothers and Daughters*, 62–4, 79–80.

34 Sergei Nechaev, "Katekhizis revoliutsionera" (1869), online at http://www.hist.msu.ru/ER/Etext/nechaev.htm. English translation at https://www.marxists.org/subject/anarchism/nechayev/catechism.htm.

35 V. Zasulich, *Vospominaniia* (Moscow: Izd. Politkatorzhan, 1931). Important parts of her memoirs are translated in Barbara Alpern Engel and Clifford N. Rosenthal, eds. and trans., *Five Sisters: Women Against the Tsar: The Memoirs of Five Young Anarchist Women of the 1870s* (London: Weidenfeld and Nicolson, 1975), 59–94.

36   G. A. Gallanin, ed., *Protsess Very Zasulich: sud i posle suda* (St. Petersburg: Sovremennik, [1906]), 34, 47–9, 75–80, 83, 87.

37   Barbara Evans Clements, *Bolshevik Feminist: The Life of Aleksandra Kollontai* (Bloomington: Indiana University Press, 1979); Beatrice Farnsworth, *Aleksandra Kollontai: Socialism, Feminism, and the Bolshevik Revolution* (Stanford: Stanford University Press, 1980); Cathy Porter, *Alexandra Kollontai: A Biography* (London: Virago, 1980; revised edition: Chicago: Haymarket, 2014).

38   Quoted in Clements, *Bolshevik Feminist*, 21.

39   A. Kollontai, "Kto takie sotsial-demokraty i chego oni khotiat?" (1906) and "K voprosu o klassovoi bor'be" (1905), both in Kollontai, *Izbrannye stat'i i rechi* (Moscow: Politizdat, 1972), 15–44; "Problemy nravstennosti s pozitivnoi tochki zreniia," *Obrazovanie*, no. 9 (September 1905): 77–95; no. 10 (October 1905): 92–107; "Etika i sotsial-demokratiia," *Obrazovanie*, no. 2 (February 1906): pt. 2, 28–32.

40   A. Kollontai, *Sotsial'nye osnovy zhenskogo voprosa* (St. Petersburg: Znanie, 1909), 109–10.

41   From essays originally published in 1911, in *Novaia moral' i rabochii klass* (Moscow: Izd. VTsIK Sovetov R. K. i K. Deputatov, 1918), quotations 40–1, 51. For translations of many of Kollontai's writings, see Holt, ed., *Selected Writings of Alexandra Kollontai*.

42   From my survey of the Moscow and St. Petersburg dailies *Rech'*, *Novoe vremia*, and *Russkoe slovo* in 1913. See also Laura Engelstein and Stephanie Sandler, eds., *Self and Story in Russian History* (Ithaca: Cornell University Press, 2000).

43   For sources, Mark Steinberg, "Worker-Authors and the Cult of the Person," in Stephen Frank and Mark Steinberg, eds., *Cultures in Flux: Lower-Class Values, Practices, and Resistance in Late Imperial Russia* (Princeton: Princeton University Press, 1994), 168–84.

44   Both quotations are by baking workers in their trade union papers: N. E. Dodaev, "Trud," *Zhizn' pekarei*, March 10, 1914: 2; M. Savin, "Bor'ba," *Bulochnik*, February 19, 1906: 5. For many examples, see Steinberg, *Proletarian Imagination*, 73–101.

45   See Anatolii Lunacharskii, *Etiudi kriticheskie i polemicheskie* (Moscow: Pravda, 1905), especially "Voprosy morali M. Meterlink" (1904), 154–78 (quotation 175–6). For a discussion of Russian Marxist view on the relationship between the individual and the collective, see Daniela Steila, "The Bolshevik 'Philosophers of Collectivism' and the Russian Revolution of 1917" (forthcoming).

Notes

46 "Ot Proletkul'ta," *Poeziia rabochego udara* (Petrograd: Proletkul't, 1918), 3.

47 Vladimir Mayakovsky, "The Fifth International" (1922), online at http://az.lib.ru/m/majakowskij_w_w/text_0340.shtml

48 M. Gor'kii, "O starom i novom cheloveke," *Pravda*, April 27, 1932, 2. Also published the same day in *Izvestiia* and in English as "The Old Gods and the New," *The New Statesman and Nation* (London, May 14, 1932), 642–5.

49 Maksim Gor'kii, *Nesvoevremennye mysli*, May 2, 1917. There are various print and online editions of the Russian, as the newspaper essays were later gathered into a book. For an English translation, Maxim Gorky, *Untimely Thoughts* (New Haven: Yale University Press, 1995). I cite the original date of publication in *Novaia zhizn'*.

50 Gor'kii, *Nesvoevremennye mysli*, April 23, 1917.

51 Ibid., November 7, 1917.

52 Ibid., December 19, 1917.

53 Maksim Gor'kii, *Foma Gordeev*, first published in the journal *Zhizn'* (Life) in 1899, online at http://az.lib.ru/g/gorxkij_m/text_0001.shtml

54 Gor'kii, "Chelovek," 211–19.

55 Gor'kii, "Ispoved."

56 Maxim Gor'kii, "Tovarishcham rabochim," *Novaia zhizn'*, July 2(15), 1917.

57 N. F. Fedorov, *What Was Man Created For? The Philosophy of the Common Task,* ed. and trans. Elisabeth Koutaissof and Marilyn Minto (London: Honeyglen, 1990); Irene Masing-Delic, *Abolishing Death: A Salvation Myth of Russian Twentieth-Century Russian Literature* (Stanford: Stanford University Press, 1992); Young, *The Russian Cosmists*; Groys, ed., *Russian Cosmism*. For the continuation of these ideas, see Anya Bernstein, *The Future of Immortality: Remaking Life and Death in Contemporary Russia* (Princeton: Princeton University Press, 2019).

58 Masing-Delic, *Abolishing Death;* Nikolai Krementsov, *A Martian Stranded on Earth: Alexander Bogdanov, Blood Transfusions, and Proletarian Science* (Chicago University of Chicago Press, 2011) and especially his *Revolutionary Experiments: The Quest for Immortality in Bolshevik Science and Fiction* (New York: Oxford University Press, 2014); Daniela Steila, "Death and Anti-Death in Russian Marxism," in *Death and Anti-Death. Volume 1: One Hundred Years After N. F. Fedorov* (Palo Alto: Ria University Press, 2003), 101–30.

59   For a recent discussion of the category of "new Soviet person," see Anna
     Krylova, "Imagining Socialism in the Soviet Century," *Social History*, 42,
     no. 3 (2017): 315–41.

60   N. Torba, "Neravenstvo i nasilie," *Griadushchee*, no. 5–6 (1920): 16–17.

61   V. Kirillov, "My," *Griadushchee*, no. 2 (May 1918): 4.

62   See Rolf Hellebust, *Flesh to Metal: Soviet Literature and the Alchemy
     of Revolution* (Ithaca: Cornell University Press, 2003); Steinberg,
     Proletarian Imagination, chaps. 4–5.

63   For example, the collection of essays and speeches put together by E.
     Iaroslavskii, *Kakim dolzhen byt' kommunist: staraia i novaia moral'*
     (Moscow: Molodaia gvardiia, 1925).

64   Jochen Hellbeck, *Revolution on My Mind: Writing a Diary Under Stalin*
     (Cambridge, MA: Harvard University Press, 2006).

65   *Piatyi vserossiiskii s'ezd VLKSM: stenograficheskii otchet, 11-19 oktiabria
     1922* (Moscow: VLKSM, 1927), 22–9, 109–60.

66   Collected as L. Trotskii, *Voprosy byta* (Moscow: Gosizdat, 1923); Leon
     Trotsky, *Problems of Everyday Life* (New York: Pathfinder, 1973).

67   Trotskii, "Bor'ba za kulturnost' rechi," in *Voprosy byta*, from *Pravda*,
     May 16, 1923; Trotsky, *Problems of Everyday Life*, 52–6.

68   Trotskii, "Neskol'ko slov o vospitanii cheloveka" (1924) online at http://
     www.magister.msk.ru/library/trotsky/trotl933.htm; Trotsky, *Problems of
     Everyday Life*, 140.

69   See, for example, Anne Gorsuch, *Youth in Revolutionary Russia:
     Enthusiasts, Bohemians, Delinquents* (Bloomington, IN: Indiana
     University Press, 2000); Elizabeth Wood, *Performing Justice: Agitation
     Trials in Early Soviet Russia* (Ithaca: Cornell University Press, 2005);
     Natalia Lebina, *Povsednevnaia zhizn' sovetskogo goroda: normy i
     anomlii, 1920–30gg.* (St. Petersburg: Neva, 1999). Komsomol archives
     and newspapers are filled with these stories and campaigns (from my
     current research on urban moralities in the 1920s and 1930s).

70   Andy Willimott, *Living the Revolution: Urban Communes and Soviet
     Socialism, 1917-1932* (Oxford: Oxford University Press, 2016), esp. chap. 3.

71   Among many explicit uses of the metaphor, see L. Trotskii, "Ot staroi
     semi'i—k novoi," *Pravda* (July 13, 1923): 2. On the centrality of moral
     thinking in Communist "millenarianism," see Slezkine, *The House of
     Government*.

72   L. Trotskii, *Literatura i revoliutsiia* (Moscow: Politizdat, 1991; orig.
     1923), 196–7.

Notes

73 L. Trotskii, "O pessimizme, optimizme, XX stoletii i mnogom drugom," *Vostochnoe obozrenie*, February 17, 1901, online at http://www.magister. msk.ru/library/trotsky/trotl457.htm.

Chapter 3

1   "Decree on the Monuments of the Republic" (April 12, 1918), including facsimile of hand-corrected original, Guerman, *Art of the October Revolution,* 8.

2   N. Punin, *Pamiatnik III internatsionala* (Petersburg: Izd. Otdela Izobrazitel'nykh iskusstv N. K. P., 1920).

3   *Izvestiia VTsIK*, August 2, 1918, 3.

4   John Milner, *Vladimir Tatlin and the Russian Avant-Garde* (New Haven: Yale University Press, 1983), 170.

5   Punin, *Pamiatnik*, 1–4.

6   Julia Bekman Chadaga, *Optical Play: Glass, Vision, and Spectacle in Russian Culture* (Evanston, IL: Northwestern University Press, 2014), esp. chap. 4.

7   Milner, *Vladimir Tatlin*, 180.

8   Italo Calvino, *Invisible Cities*, trans. William Weaver (New York: Harcourt, 1974), 2, 44.

9   Burton Pike, *The Image of the City in Modern Literature* (Princeton: Princeton University Press, 1981); Robert Alter, *Imagined Cities: Urban Experience and the Language of the Novel* (New Haven: Yale University Press, 2005).

10 Lewis Mumford, *The Story of Utopias* (New York: Boni and Liveright, 1922), 11.

11 Nathaniel Coleman, *Utopias and Architecture* (London: Routledge, 2005), 5.

12 Bloch, *The Principle of Hope*, II: 699–745.

13 The literature on the Petersburg Text in Russian cultural history is huge. Two influential works are N. P. Antsiferov, "*Nepostizhimyi gorod . . .*": *Dusha Peterburga. Peterburg Dostoevskogo. Peterburg Pushkina*, ed. M. B. Verblovskaia (St. Petersburg: Lenizdat, 1991, originally published in the 1920s) and V. N. Toporov, *Peterburgskii tekst russkoi literatury: izbrannye trudy* (St. Petersburg: Iskusstvo-SPB, 2003). For studies in English, see especially Katerina Clark, *Petersburg, Crucible of Revolution*

(Cambridge, MA: Harvard University Press, 1995) and Julie Buckler, *Mapping St. Petersburg: Imperial Text and Cityshape* (Princeton: Princeton University Press, 2005).

14 Fedor Dostoevskii, "Peterburgskaia letopis," in *Sanktpeterburgskie vedomosti*, April 27, May 11, June 1, and June 15, 1847, in F. M. Dostoevskii, *Sobranie sochinenii v piatnadtsati tomakh* (Leningrad-St. Petersburg: Nauka, 1988–1996), 2:5–33.

15 Dostoevskii, *Prestuplenie i nakazanie*, pt. II, chap. 6, pt. VI, chaps. 3 and 6.

16 See the Introduction.

17 A. Karelin, "K voprosu o psikhike proletariev: eksiz," *Sovremennik* 1912, no. 3 (March): 282–95, esp. 284–6.

18 Aleks. Mertvago, "Peterburg i Moskva," *Rech'*, August 26, 1907, 3.

19 G. Tsyperovich, "Kinematograf," *Sovremennyi mir*, no. 1 (January 1912): 181.

20 Favn, "Malen'kii fel'eton: 'Neo'. . .," *Novoe vremia*, May 20, 1909, 4.

21 Sluchainyi, "Nazad ili vpered," *Gazeta-kopeika*, June 27, 1910, 4–5.

22 N. Valentinov, "Gorod i gorozhane," *Novyi zhurnal dlia vsekh* 1910, no. 20 (June): 91–6.

23 Catriona Kelly and David Shepherd, eds., *Constructing Russian Culture in the Age of Revolution: 1881-1940* (Oxford: Oxford University Press, 1998); Louise McReynolds, *Russia at Play: Leisure Activities at the End of the Tsarist Era* (Ithaca: Cornell University Press, 2003); Steinberg, *Petersburg Fin de Siècle*.

24 Steinberg, *Petersburg Fin de Siècle*, 199–211.

25 Charles Baudelaire, *Le Peintre de la Vie Moderne* (1863), in *The Painter of Modern Life and Other Essays*, trans. and ed. Jonathan Mayne (London: Phaidon, 1964), 9.

26 M. Kalinin review of *Sbornik proletarskikh pisatelei* (1914), *Rabochii*, June 23, 1914, reprinted in *Dooktiabr'skaia "Pravda" ob iskusstve i literature* (Moscow: Gos. izdatel'stvo "Khudozhestvennaia literatura." 1937), 39.

27 V. Polianskii, "Motivy rabochei poezii," *Proletarskaia kul'tura*, no. 3 (August 1918): 5.

28 See Steinberg, *Proletarian Imagination*, chap. 4, where I quote and analyze many examples.

29 This composite is made from fragments taken from workers' verses published between 1905 and 1917 in *Pervyi sbornik proletarskikh pisatelei* (St. Petersburg: Priboi, 1914); *Sbornik proletarskikh pisatalei*, ed.

M. Gor'kii, A. Serebrov, and A. Chapygin (Petrograd: Parus, 1917); and a variety of socialist and trade union newspapers. The translations are mine.

30   From *Pervyi sbornik proletarskikh pisatelei*; *Pod znamia pravdy: pervyi sbornik obshchestva proletarskikh iskusstv* (Petersburg [*sic*]: Priboi, 1917); *Poeziia v bol'shevistskikh izdaniiakh, 1901-1917* (Leningrad: Sovetskii pisatel', 1967); and various socialist and labor newspapers of the time. The translations are mine.

31   Trotskii, "O pessimizme, optimizme, XX stoletii i mnogom drugom."

32   Antonio Gramsci, "Discorso agli anarchici," *L'Ordine Nuovo* (April 3–10, 1920), 340. Gramsci is quoting Romain Rolland. See Antonio Gramsci, *Prison Notebooks*, ed. and trans. Joseph Buttigieg, 3 vols. (New York: Columbia University Press, 1991–2007), vol. 1: 474–5.

33   Quotations from influential Bolshevik cultural leaders: Polianskii, "Motivy rabochei poezii," V. L. L'vovRogachevskii, *Ocherki proletarskoi literatury* (Moscow-Leningrad: Moskovskoe akts. izdatel'skoe obshchestvo, 1927), 110–11; and A. Voronskii, *Iskusstvo i zhizn': sbornik statei* (Moscow and Petrograd: Krug, 1924), 128–32.

34   Phrases from various poems, especially V. Aleksandrovskii, "Iz tsikla 'Moskva,'" *Tvori!*, no. 1 (December 1920): 4; V. Kirillov, "Gorodu," *Griadushchee*, no. 2 (May 1918): 6; Ia. Berdnikov, "Gorod," *Griadushchee*, no. 12–13 (1920): 1.

35   I. Filipchenko, "Lenin," *Rabochii zhurnal*, no. 1 (1924): 65.

36   N. Liashko, "O zadachakh pisatelia-rabochego," *Kuznitsa*, no. 3 (July 1920): 27–9.

37   N. Liashko, "Dukhovnye iady goroda i kooperatsiia," *Rabochii mir* 1918, no. 7 (June 23): 24–5.

38   The quoted words are from V. Aleksandrovskii, "Moskva (otryvki iz poemy)," *Kuznitsa*, no. 5 (October–November 1920): 12–16. For a discussion of the realities and public responses to urban life in the wake of the 1917 revolution, see Mark D. Steinberg, *The Russian Revolution, 1905-21* (Oxford: Oxford University Press, 2017), 138–59.

39   N. Liashko, "O byte i literature perekhodnogo vremeni," *Kuznitsa*, no. 8 (April–September 1921): 29.

40   See S. Frederick Starr, "Visionary Town Planning During the Cultural Revolution," in *Cultural Revolution in Russia, 1928-1931*, ed. Sheila Fitzpatrick (Bloomington: Indiana University Press, 1978), 207–40; Richard Stites, *Revolutionary Dreams: Utopian Vision and Experimental Life in the Russian Revolution* (New York: Oxford University Press,

1989), chap. 9; Stephen Kotkin, *Magnetic Mountain: Stalinism as Civilization* (Berkeley: University of California Press, 1995); Evgeny Dobrenko and Eric Naiman, eds., *Landscape of Stalinism: The Art and Ideology of Soviet Space* (Seattle: University of Washington Press, 2003); Karl Schlögel, *Moscow* (London: Reaktion, 2004); Katerina Clark, *Moscow, the Fourth Rome; Stalinism, Cosmopolitanism, and the Evolution of Soviet Culture* (Cambridge, MA: Harvard University Press, 2011); Slezkine, *The House of Government*, esp. chap. 6.

41 See Chapter 4.

42 S. Frederick Starr, *Melnikov: Solo Architect in a Mass Society* (Princeton: Princeton University Press, 1978), 148–9.

43 In addition to his famous book, *The City in History* (1961), see Lewis Mumford, "What Is a City," *Architectural Record* (1937), reprinted in numerous collections and online.

44 N. A. Miliutin, *Sotsgorod: Problemy stroitel'stva sotsialisticheskikh gorodov* (Moscow: Gosizdat, 1930), esp. 9–18.

45 Starr, "Visionary Town Planning," 207–11; L. M. Sabsovich, *SSSR cherez 15 let* (Moscow: Planovoe khoziastvo, 1929), esp. 129–30; L. Sabsovich, "Pochemy my dolzhnyi i mozhem stroit' sotsialisticheskie goroda?" *Revoliutsiia i kul'tura*, no. 1 (January 15, 1930), esp. 21–4.

46 M. Okhitovich, "Sotsialisticheskii sposob rasseleniia i sotsialisticheskii tip zhil'ia," *Vestnik kommunisticheskoi akademii*, no. 35–6 (1929): esp. pp. 337–8.

47 *Sovremennaia arkhitektura*, no. 1–2 (1930): 4–6, 11, online at http://teh ne.com/library/sovremennaya-arhitektura-zhurnal-1926-1930.

48 M. Okhitovich, "Zametki po teorii rasseleniia," *Sovremennaia arkhitektura*, no. 1–2 (1930): 13.

49 Mikhail Barsch and Moisei Ginzburg, "Zelenyi gorod," *Sovremennaia arkhitektura*, no. 1–2 (1930): 20–37. On one of Ginzburg's most important completed buildings, see Victor Buchli, *An Archeology of Socialism* (Oxford: Berg, 1999).

50 Selim Omarovich Khan-Magomedov, *Georgii Krutikov: The Flying City and Beyond* [2008], trans. Christina Lodder (Barcelona: Tenov, 2015); Alla Vronskaya, "Two Utopias of Georgii Krutikov's City of the Future," *Writing Cities (London School of Economics and Political Science Working Papers)*, Vol. 2: *Distance and Cities*, (2012), 51–2.

51 *Postroika*, July 3, 1928, cited in Khan-Magomedov, *Georgii Krutikov*.

52 Vronskaya, "Two Utopias"; Mumford, *The Story of Utopias*, 14–15.

53 See also Julia Vaingurt, *Wonderlands of the Avant-Garde: Technology and the Arts in Russia of the 1920s* (Evanston: Northwestern University Press, 2013), 13, 226.

54 Khan-Magomedov, *Georgii Krutikov*, esp. 46–69; Vronskaya, "Two Utopias," 46–56.

55 S. M. Kirov, *Izbrannye stat'i i rechi, 1912-1934* (Leningrad: Gosudarstvennoe izdatel'stvo politicheskoi literatury, 1939), 178.

56 Starr, *Melnikov*, 156–61.

57 Clark, *Moscow*, 94–104.

58 Mikhail Ryklin, "'The Best in the World': The Discourse of the Moscow Metro in the 1930s," in Dobrenko and Naiman, eds., *Landscape of Stalinism*, 264–66.

59 Clark, *Moscow*, 97–8; Slezkine, *House of Government*, 318–28, 357–62; Maria Kostyuk, *Boris Iofan: Architect Behind the Palace of the Soviets* (Berlin: DOM, 2019).

60 For an influential examination of the complex relationship between Soviet architecture of the 1920s and 1930s, and of the competing political cultures fueling these, see Vladimir Paperny, *Architecture in the Age of Stalin: Culture Two* (Cambridge: Cambridge University Press, 2002).

61 The most influential theorists, of course, are Edmund Burke and Immanuel Kant. In architecture, discussions of the sublime are also influenced by Jean-Francois Lyotard. For some key discussions of the sublime in Soviet cultural history, especially architecture, see Buck-Morss, *Dreamworld and Catastrophe*, 180–1; Clark, *Moscow*, 276–306; Schlögel, *Moscow*, 72; and Vaingurt, *Wonderlands*, 129.

62 Slezkine, *House of Government*, 359.

63 Schlögel, *Moscow*, 72–3

64 Buck-Morss, *Dreamworld and Catastrophe*, 180–1.

65 As discussed by Buck-Morss, *Dreamworld and Catastrophe*, 181–2. For discussions of the ongoing histories of destruction, loss, resistance, preservation, and memory in late-Soviet and post-Soviet urban Russia, see Stephen V. Bittner, *The Many Lives of Khrushchev's Thaw: Experience and Memory in Moscow's Arbat* (Ithaca: Cornell University Press, 2008) and Catriona Kelly, *St Petersburg: Shadows of the Past* (New Haven: Yale University Press, 2014).

66 Stites, *Revolutionary Dreams*, chap. 11.

67 Clark, *Moscow*, 125.

Chapter 4

1   S. V. Mironenko, ed., *Dnevniki imperatora Nikolaia (1894-1918)* vol. 1 (Moscow: ROSSPEN, 2011), 711–12, 776; Sofiia Buksgevden, *Ventsenosnaia muchenitsa: Zhizn' i tragediia Aleksandry Feodorovny* (Moscow: Russkii khronograf, 2006), 165–7; *Sankt-Peterburgskie vedomosti*, February 13 (26), 1903, 3 and February 15, 1903, 3–4.

2   *Tsarskoe prebyvanie v Moskve v aprele 1900 goda* (St. Petersburg: Tip. br. Panteleevykh, 1900), 55–6; L. G. Zakharova, "Krizis samoderzhaviia nakanune revoliutsii 1905 goda," *Voprosy istorii*, no. 8 (August 1972): 131.

3   For a richly detailed and insightful account, see Richard Wortman, *Scenarios of Power: Myth and Ceremony in Russian Monarchy*, 2 vols, vol. 2 (Princeton: Princeton University Press, 1995), 200, chap. 13.

4   V. O. Kliuchevskii, *Kurs russkoi istorii*, Lecture XLIV, in *Sochineniia v deviati tomakh*, vol. 3 (Moscow: Mysl', 1988), 62–5; Wortman, *Scenarios of Power*, 2:439–40.

5   A. Elchaninov, *Tsarstvovanie Gosudaria Imperatora Nikolaia Aleksandrovicha* (St. Petersburg and Moscow: T-vo. N. D. Sytina, 1913), 115, 134; idem., *The Tsar and His People* (London: Hodder & Stoughton, 1914), 121, 148.

6   *Tsarskoe prebyvanie*; Wortman, *Scenarios of Power*, 2:476 (quotation).

7   See the recollections of his prime minister, Vladimir N. Kokovtsov, *Out of My Past: The Memoirs of Count Kokovtsov* (Stanford: Stanford University Press, 1935), 360–1.

8   Andrew M. Verner, *The Crisis of the Russian Autocracy: Nicholas II and the 1905 Revolution* (Princeton: Princeton University Press, 1990); Dominic Lieven, *Nicholas II: Emperor of All the Russias* (London: St. Martins, 1993); Mark D. Steinberg and Vladimir M. Khrustalev, *Fall of the Romanovs: Political Dreams and Personal Struggles in a Time of Revolution* (New Haven: Yale University Press, 1995), Introduction and *passim*.

9   Steinberg and Khrustalev, *Fall of the Romanovs*, 20 (quotation) and *passim*.

10 *Pravitel'stvennyi vestnik*, January 20 (February 2), 1906 and April 28 (May 11), 1906.

11 *The Russian Primary Chronicle*, ed. and trans. Samuel Hazzard Cross and Olgerd P. Sherbowitz-Witzor (Cambridge: Medieval Academy of America, 1953), 59.

Notes

12 For a detailed exploration of this theme in Russian history, though the phrase is mine, see Wortman, *Scenarios of Power.*

13 Catherine II, *Nakaz Kommissii o sochinenii proekta novogo ulozheniia* (Moscow: Pechatano pri Senate, 1767), online at https://www.prlib.ru/item/428545, Articles, 6, 7, 13, 34, 521.

14 Quoted in R. V. Ovchinnikov, "Sledsvtie i sud nad E. I. Pugachev," *Voprosy istorii* 1966, no. 3 (March): 126.

15 Wortman, *Scenarios of Power*, 1:233.

16 Correspondance de l'empereur Alexandre Ier avec sa soeur la grande duchesse Catherine princesse d'Oldenbourg (St. Petersburg, Manufacture des papiers de l'etat, 1910), 32–3.

17 Richard Pipes, "The Russian Military Colonies, 1810–1831," *Journal of Modern History*, 22, no. 3 (September 1950): 209–10, 215. See also Stites, *Revolutionary Dreams*, 21–3; Wortman, *Scenarios of Power*, 1:232–4.

18 Dal', *Tolkovyi slovar' zhivogo velikorusskogo iazyka*, "samoderzhavie."

19 Nikolai Karamzin, *Karamzin's Memoir on Ancient and Modern Russia: A Translation and Analysis*, ed. Richard Pipes. New edition (Ann Arbor: University of Michigan Press, 2005), 118, 139.

20 Cynthia H. Whittaker, *The Origins of Modern Russian Education: An Intellectual Biography of Count Sergei Uvarov, 1786-1855* (DeKalb: Northern Illinois University Press, 1984), 4.

21 Nicholas Riasanovsky, *Nicholas I and Official Nationality in Russia, 1825-1855* (Berkeley: University of California Press, 1959), 135.

22 Nicholas I, "Manifesto of July 13, 1826," in *Polnoe sobranie zakonov Rossiiskoi imperii. Sobranie vtoroe* (St. Petersburg: Pechatano v Tip. II Otd. Sobstvennoi ego Imperatorskago Velichestva Kantselarii, 1825–1881), vol. 1 (1825–26), no. 465 (pp. 772–3).

23 Riasanovsky, *Nicholas I*, 73–183; Whittaker, *Origins of Modern Russian Education*, 103–8.

24 "Ustav soiuza blagodenstviia" [1816], *Izbrannye proizvedeniia sotsial'no-politicheskie i filosofskie proizvedeniia dekabristov*, ed. I. Ia. Shchipanov, 3 vols (Moscow: Gos. izdatel'stvo politicheskoi literatury, 1951), I:237–76; Marc Raeff, ed., *The Decembrist Movement* (Englewood Cliffs, NJ: Prentice-Hall, 1966), 69–99.

25 N. M. Murav'ev, "Proekt Konstitutsii," *Izbrannye proizvedeniia dekabristov* I:296–987; Raeff, *Decembrist Movement*, 103–5.

26 P. I. Pestel, "Russkaia Pravda," *Izbrannye proizvedeniia dekabristov*
    II:76–7; Raeff, *Decembrist Movement*, 125–6.

27 Raeff, *Decembrist Movement*, 45–56.

28 See the Introduction.

29 A. D. Ulybyshev, "Son," *Izbrannye proizvedeniia dekabristov* I:286–92;
    Raeff, *Decembrist Movement*, 60–6.

30 See, especially, William G. Rosenberg, *Liberals in the Russian
    Revolution: The Constitutional Democratic Party, 1917-1921* (Princeton:
    Princeton University Press, 1974).

31 "Chetvertaia rech' Bakunina na kongresse Ligi Mira i Svobody v
    1868 g.," in M. A. Bakunin, *Stat'ia Gertsena o Bakunina, Biograficheskii
    ocherk M. Dragomanova, Rechi i vozzvaniia* (St. Petersburg: Izd.
    Balashova, 1906), 206–7.

32 Among many books on anarchism, see, for example, Paul Avrich,
    Russian Anarchists (Princeton: Princeton University Press, 1967); James
    Joll, *The Anarchists*, second edition (Cambridge, MA: Harvard University
    Press, 1979); Peter Marshall, *Demanding the Impossible: A History of
    Anarchism* (London: Harper Collins, 1992); Colin Ward, *Anarchism: A
    Very Short Introduction* (Oxford: Oxford University Press, 2004).

33 Peter Kropotkin, "Anarchism," *Encyclopedia Britannica*, vol. 1, 11th
    edition (Cambridge: Encyclopedia Britannica, 1910), 914.

34 M. A. Bakunin, *Sobranie sochinenii i pisem 1828-1876*, ed. Iu. M. Steklov
    (Moscow: Izd. Obshchestva Politkatorzhan, 1934–5), 3 volumes, I:154.
    See also Franco Venturi, *Roots of Revolution: A History of the Popular
    and Socialist Movements in Nineteenth Century Russia* (New York:
    Knopf, 1960), 37. On the Bakunin family idyll, see Randolph, *The House
    in the Garden.*

35 A biography of Bakunin that speaks of the "psychology of utopianism,"
    though with a different definition and interpretation than mine, is
    Aileen Kelly, *Mikhail Bakunin: A Study in the Psychology and Politics
    of Utopianism* (New Haven: Yale University Press, 1987). See also E. H.
    Carr, *Michael Bakunin* (London: Macmillan, 1937).

36 Quoted in Venturi, *Roots of Revolution*, 47.

37 Bakunin, *Sobranie sochinenii*, III:249–50.

38 Jules Elysard [Mikhail Bakunin], "Die Reaktion in Deutschland
    (Ein Fragment von einem Franzosen)," in *Deutsche Jahrbücher fur
    Wissenschaft and Kunst*, October 17–21, 1842, online at https://anarchi
    stischebibliothek.org/library/die-reaktion-in-deutschland.

Notes

39 M. Bakunin, "Federalism, Socialism, Anti-theologism" (1867), online at https://www.marxists.org/reference/archive/bakunin/works/various/reasons-of-state.htm

40 "Chetvertaia rech'" (1868), in Bakunin, *Rechi i vozzvaniia* (St. Petersburg: Balashova, 1906), 206–7.

41 *Statism and Anarchy* (1873), in Mikhail Aleksandrovich Bakunin, *Izbrannye trudy*, ed. P. I. Talerov and A. A. Shiriniants (Moscow: ROSSPEN, 2010), 486.

42 Karl Marx, "Political Indifferentism" (1874), online at https://www.marxists.org/archive/marx/works/1873/01/indifferentism.htm

43 Friedrich Engels, "On Authority," (1874), online at https://www.marxists.org/archive/marx/works/1872/10/authority.htm

44 Karl Marx, *Eighteenth Brumaire of Louis Napoleon* (1851–2), online at https://www.marxists.org/archive/marx/works/1852/18th-brumaire/ch07.htm

45 V. I. Lenin, *State and Revolution* (1917). Russian: Lenin, *Izbrannye proizvedeniia v chetryekh tomakh* (Moscow, Gos. izdatel'stvo politicheskoi literatury, 1988), 2:321–410. English: https://www.marxists.org/archive/lenin/works/1917/staterev/. For a lively and knowledgeable history of Lenin's life and ideas, see Lars Lih, *Lenin* (London: Reaktion, 2011).

46 Lenin summarizes Marx's *The Civil War in France*, online at https://www.marxists.org/archive/marx/works/1871/civil-war-france/

47 Lenin, "Can the Bolsheviks Retain State Power," *Izbrannye proizvedeniia* 2:399–406. Note: for accessibility, in the notes following, I will give the titles of Lenin's works in English (they are widely available) and the Russian source I used.

48 "To the Population," November 5, 1917, *Pravda*, November 6, 1917; "How to Organize Competition" (written December 24–27, 1917 but unpublished at the time); and "The Immediate Tasks of Soviet Power," *Pravda*, April 28, 1918, in Russian in Lenin, *Izbrannye proizvedeniia* 3:24, 48, 165.

49 Orlando Figes, *A People's Tragedy: The Russian Revolution, 1891-1924* (Harmondsworth: Penguin, 1996), 503.

50 Lenin, "Fright at the Fall of the Old and the Fight for the New" (written December 24–27, 1917), first published *Pravda*, January 22, 1929, 1; "How to Organize Competition" (written December 24–27, 1917), *Pravda*, January 22, 1929, 1; "The Immediate Tasks of Soviet Power" (April 1918), *Izbrannye proizvedeniia*, 3:162–92.

51 Lenin, "Telegram to Penza Communists" (August 11, 1918), in Richard Pipes, ed., *The Unknown Lenin: From the Secret Archive* (New Haven: Yale University Press, 1998), 50–2 (including photo of original text).

52 Lenin, "Fright at the Fall of the Old and the Fight for the New." See also James Ryan, *Lenin's Terror: The Ideological Origins of Early State Violence* (New York: Routledge, 2012), 86–8, 97–8.

53 Emma Goldman, *My Disillusionment in Russia* (London: C.W. Daniel, 1925), quotes 61, 251.

54 Lenin, Speech at the 10th Party Congress, March 8, 1921, *Pravda*, March 10, 1921, 1–2.

55 Mark D. Steinberg, *Voices of Revolution, 1917* (New Haven: Yale University Press, 2001); idem., *The Russian Revolution, 1905-21.*

56 Letter to Minister of Justice Alexander Kerensky from A. Zemskov, March 26, 1917. State Archive of the Russian Federation (GARF), f. 6978, op. 1, d. 296, ll. 39-45ob, in Steinberg, *Voices of Revolution*, 85–91.

57 Report to Kerensky from peasants in Valdaisk uezd, Novgorod Province, August 19, 1917, GARF, f. 1778, op. 1, d. 363, ll. 244-44ob, in Steinberg, *Voices of Revolution*, 239–40.

58 Afinogenov (representing the Ouf Metal Plant), speech to Third Conference of Petrograd Factory Committees, September 10, 1917, in *Oktiabr'skaia revoliutsiia i fabzavkomy*, part 2 (Moscow: Izd. VTsSPS, 1927), 23. Also quoted in Paul Avrich, ed., *The Anarchists in the Russian Revolution* (Ithaca: Cornell University Press, 1973), 88.

59 *Golos Truda*, November–December 1917, in Avrich, *Anarchists*, 96–106.

60 Nestor Makhno, "Manifesto," in Avrich, *Anarchists*, 128.

61 "Declaration of the Revolutionary Insurrectionary Army of Ukraine (Makhnovists)" (in Russian), January 7, 1920, in "Proclamations of the Machno [sic] Movement, 1920," ed. L. J. van Rossum, *International Review of Social History*, 13, no. 2 (1968): 252–4. Also in Avrich, *Anarchists*, 133–5.

62 "Stop! Read! Consider!" (in Russian), June 1920, *International Review of Social History*, 13, no. 2 (1968): 268; Avrich, *Anarchists*, 137.

63 See, for example, also Igor' Narskii, *Zhizn' v katastrofe: Budni naseleniia v 1917-1922 gg.* (Moscow: ROSSPEN, 2001).

64 Lenin, "Report on the Substitution of a Tax in Kind for the Surplus Grain Appropriation System," March 15, 1921, *Pravda*, March 16, 1921.

65 Nikolai Sukhanov, *Letopis' revoliutsii*, vol. 4 (Berlin and Moscow: Izd. Z. I. Grzhebina, 1922), 424–5.

Notes

66   Resolution approved at mass meeting, March 1, 1921, *Izvestiia
Vremennogo revoliutsionnogo komiteta matrosov, krasnoarmeitsev,
i rabochikh* (the paper of the Kronstadt Provisional Revolutionary
Committee), March 3, 1921, in V. P. Naumov and A. A Kosakovskii,
Kronshtadt 1921 (Moscow: Mezhdunarodnyi fond "Demokratiia," 1997),
50–1. Also Avrich, *Anarchists*, 158–9 and https://upload.wikimedia.org/
wikipedia/commons/e/e3/19210301-kronstadt_resolution.jpg.

67   Avrich, *Anarchists*, 156.

68   "Za chto my boremsia," *Izvestiia Vremennogo revoliutsionnogo komiteta*,
March 8, 1921, 1, online at http://nlr.ru/res/inv/ukazat55/record_full.ph
p?record_ID=155754; Avrich, *Anarchists*, 159–61.

69   "Vlast' sovetam, a ne partiiam!" *Izvestiia Vremennogo revoliutsionnogo
komiteta*, March 15, 1921, in Naumov and Kosakovskii, *Kronshtadt*,
141–2.

70   The classic study is Robert V. Daniels, *The Conscience of the Revolution:
Communist Opposition in Soviet Russia* (Cambridge, MA: Harvard
University Press, 1960).

71   R. Abramovich at the Third Congress of Trade Unions, in Isaac
Deutscher, *The Prophet Armed: Trotsky, 1879-1921* (Oxford: Oxford
University Press, 1954), 500.

72   "Tezisy rabochei oppozitsii," *Pravda*, January 25, 1921, 2–3, also online
at http://www.marxists.org/archive/shliapnikov/1921/workers-oppositi
on.htm.

73   From debates at the Tenth Party Congress, March 1921, quoted and
discussed in Deutscher, *The Prophet Armed*, 508–10.

74   *Rabochaia oppozitsiia* (Moscow: 8-ia Gos. tip., 1921), 15–16.

75   Ibid., 19, 24, 33, 38–9, 47.

76   Ibid., 22, 32, 35, 38–40, 48.

77   Cited by Stephen Cohen, *Bukharin and the Bolshevik Revolution: A
Political Biography, 1888-1938* (New York: Knopf, 1973), 157.

78   Speech by Stalin, "There Are No Fortresses That Bolsheviks Cannot
Storm" (in Russian), *Pravda*, February 5, 1931, 3.

79   Quoted in A. Yugow [Iugov], *Russia's Economic Front for War and Peace:
An Appraisal of the Three Five-Year Plans*, trans. from the Russian (New
York: Harper, 1942), 5–6. There is debate about the accuracy of this
quote, though not about Stalin's repeated use of the key phrase.

80   On "speaking Bolshevik," see Kotkin, *Magnetic Mountain*. On Stalin-
era subjectivities, see Hellbeck, *Revolution on My Mind* and Krylova,
"Imagining Socialism in the Soviet Century," 315–41.

81   Lyons, *Assignment in Utopia*, 240–9.

82   I. Stalin, "O zadachakh khoziaistvennikov," *Pravda*, February 5, 1931.

83   Quoted in Katerina Clark, "Little Heroes and Big Deeds," in Sheila Fitzpatrick, ed., *Cultural Revolution in Russia, 1928-1931* (Bloomington: Indiana University Press, 1978), 191–2.

Conclusion

1   Václav Havel, *The Power of the Powerless* [1978] (London: Vintage, 2018).

2   Phrases from Ernst Bloch and Walter Benjamin. See the Introduction.

3   Bloch, *The Spirit of Utopia,* 1.

4   For quotations, see the Introduction.

5   "Metaphor: The Conceptual Leap," *Critical Inquiry,* 5, no. 1 (Autumn 1978): 1–159.

6   Cited by Ivan Kubikov, writing in the newspaper of the Petersburg printers' union, of which he was a leader. *Pechatnoe delo*, 1912, no. 5 (May 11): 9.

7   Susan Buck-Morss, *Dreamworld and Catastrophe*, 62–3, 69.

8   Benjamin, "Paralipomena to 'On the Concept of History,'" *Selected Writings*, 4 vols. (Cambridge, MA, 1996–2003), 4:402.

9   Hannah Arendt, "What Is Freedom," in *Between Past and Future: Six Exercises in Political Thought* (New York: Viking, 1961), 169–71.

SELECTED FURTHER READINGS

Russian Utopia

Baehr, Stephen. *The Paradise Myth in Eighteenth-Century Russia: Utopian Patterns in Early Secular Russian Literature and Culture*. Stanford: Stanford University Press, 1991.

Bowlt, John and Olga Matich, eds. *Laboratory of Dreams: The Russian Avant-Garde and Cultural Experiment*. Stanford: Stanford University Press, 1996.

Boym, Svetlana, *Another Freedom: The Alternative History of an Idea*. Chicago: University of Chicago Press, 2010.

Buck-Morss, Susan. *Dreamworld and Catastrophe: The Passing of Mass Utopia in East and West*. Cambridge, MA: MIT Press, 2000.

Clark, Katerina. *Moscow, the Fourth Rome; Stalinism, Cosmopolitanism, and the Evolution of Soviet Culture*. Cambridge, MA: Harvard University Press, 2011.

Clark, Katerina. *Petersburg, Crucible of Cultural Revolution*. Cambridge, MA: Harvard University Press, 1995.

The Great Utopia: The Russian and Soviet Avant-Garde, 1915–1932. New York: Guggenheim Museum, 1992 (exhibition catalogue).

Gurianova, Nina. *The Aesthetics of Anarchy: Art and Ideology in the Early Russian Avant-Garde*. Berkeley: University of California Press, 2012.

Halfin, Igal. *From Darkness to Light: Class, Consciousness, and Salvation in Revolutionary Russia*. Pittsburgh: University of Pittsburgh Press, 2000.

Hellbeck, Jochen. *Revolution on My Mind: Writing a Diary Under Stalin*. Cambridge, MA: Harvard University Press, 2006.

Heller, Mikhail and Aleksandr Nekrich. *Utopia in Power: The History of the Soviet Union from 1917 to the Present*. New York: Summit Books, 1986.

Hillis, Faith. *Utopia's Discontents: Russian Exiles and the Quest for Freedom, 1830–1930*. New York: Oxford University Press, 2021.

Kelly, Aileen. *Mikhail Bakunin: A Study in the Psychology and Politics of Utopianism*. New Haven: Yale University Press, 1987.

Kelly, Aileen. *The Discovery of Chance: The Life and Thought of Alexander Herzen*. Cambridge, MA: Harvard University Press, 2016.

Kelly, Aileen. *Toward Another Shore: Russian Thinkers Between Necessity and Chance.* New Haven: Yale University Press, 1998.

Kelly, Catriona, ed. *Utopias.* Harmondsworth: Penguin, 1999.

Margolin, Victor. *The Struggle for Utopia: Rodchenko, Lissitzky, Moholy-Nagy, 1917–1946.* Chicago: University of Chicago Press, 1997.

Matich, Olga. *Erotic Utopia: The Decadent Imagination in Russia's Fin-de-Siècle.* Madison, WI: University of Wisconsin Press, 2005.

Paperno, Irina and Joan Delaney Grossman. *Creating Life: The Aesthetic Utopia of Russian Modernism.* Stanford: Stanford University Press, 1994.

Randolph, John. *The House in the Garden: the Bakunin Family and the Romance of Russian Idealism.* Ithaca: Cornell University Press, 2007.

Ree, Erik van. *Boundaries of Utopia: Imagining Communism from Plato to Stalin.* Abingdon: Routledge, 2015.

Rosenberg, William G., ed. *Bolshevik Visions: First Phase of the Cultural Revolution in Soviet Russia.* Ann Arbor: Ardis, 1990.

Rosenthal, Bernice Glatzer. *New Myth, New World: From Nietzsche to Stalinism.* University Park: Pennsylvania State University, 2002.

Slezkine, Yuri. *The House of Government: A Saga of the Russian Revolution.* Princeton: Princeton University Press, 2017.

Steinberg, Mark. *The Russian Revolution, 1905–1921.* Oxford: Oxford University Press, 2017.

Stites, Richard. *Revolutionary Dreams: Utopian Vision and Revolutionary Life in the Russian Revolution.* Oxford: Oxford University Press, 1989.

Todorova, Maria. *The Lost World of Socialists at Europe's Margins: Imagining Utopia, 1870s-1920s.* London: Bloomsbury, 2020.

Willimott, Andy. *Living the Revolution: Urban Communes and Soviet Socialism, 1917–1932.* Oxford: Oxford University Press, 2016.

The Concept of Utopia

Bloch, Ernst. *The Spirit of Utopia* (a translation of the revised 1923 German edition). Stanford: Stanford University Press, 2000.

Bloch, Ernst. *The Principle of Hope*, 3 vols. Cambridge, MA: MIT Press, 1986–1995.

Bloch, Ernst. *The Utopian Function of Art and Literature: Selected Essays*, trans. Jack Zipes and Frank Mecklenburg. Cambridge, MA: MIT Press, 1988

Claeys, Gregory. *Searching for Utopia: The History of an Idea.* New York: Thames and Hudson, 2011.

Selected Further Readings

Gordin, Michael D., Helen Tilley, and Gyan Prakash, eds. *Utopia/Dystopia: Conditions of Historical Possibility*. Princeton: Princeton University Press, 2010.

Jameson, Frederic. *Archaeologies of the Future: The Desire Called Utopia and Other Science Fictions*. London: Verso, 2005.

Levitas, Ruth. *The Concept of Utopia*. Syracuse: Syracuse University Press, 1990.

Levitas, Ruth. *Utopia as Method: The Imaginary Reconstitution of Society*. London: Palgrave Macmillan, 2013.

Löwy, Michael. *Fire Alarm: Reading Walter Benjamin's "On the Concept of History."* London: Verso, 2005.

Manuel, Frank E., and Fritzie P. Manuel. *Utopian Thought in the Western World*. Cambridge, MA: Harvard University Press, 1979.

Muñoz, José Esteban. *Cruising Utopia: The Then and There of Queer Futurity*. New York: New York University Press, 2009.

Ricoeur, Paul. *Lectures on Ideology and Utopia*, ed. George Taylor. New York: Columbia University Press, 1986.

Rüsen, Jörn, Michael Fehr, and Thomas W. Rieger. *Thinking Utopia: Steps into Other Worlds*. New York: Berghahn Books, 2005.

Sargent, Lyman Tower. *Utopianism: A Very Short Introduction*. Oxford: Oxford University Press, 2010.

Walicki, Andrzej. *Marxism and the Leap to the Kingdom of Freedom: The Rise and Fall of the Communist Utopia*. Stanford: Stanford University Press, 1995.

INDEX

Index

136

Index

9 781350 127210